WAITING ON THE SPIRIT OF PROMISE

Monographs in Baptist History

VOLUME 1

SERIES EDITOR
Michael A. G. Haykin, The Southern Baptist Theological Seminary

EDITORIAL BOARD
Matthew Barrett, The Southern Baptist Theological Seminary
Peter Beck, Charleston Southern University
Anthony L. Chute, California Baptist University
Jason G. Duesing, Southwestern Baptist Theological Seminary
Nathan A. Finn, Southeastern Baptist Theological Seminary
Crawford Gribben, Trinity College, Dublin
Gordon L. Heath, McMaster Divinity College
Barry Howson, Heritage Theological Seminary
Jason K. Lee, Southwestern Baptist Theological Seminary
Thomas J. Nettles, The Southern Baptist Theological Seminary
James A. Patterson, Union University
James M. Renihan, Institute of Reformed Baptist Studies
Jeffrey P. Straub, Central Baptist Theological Seminary
Brian R. Talbot, Broughty Ferry Baptist Church, Scotland
Malcolm B. Yarnell III, Southwestern Baptist Theological Seminary

Ours is a day in which not only the gaze of western culture but also increasingly that of Evangelicals is riveted to the present. The past seems to be nowhere in view and hence it is disparagingly dismissed as being of little value for our rapidly changing world. Such historical amnesia is fatal for any culture, but particularly so for Christian communities whose identity is profoundly bound up with their history. The goal of this new series of monographs, Studies in Baptist History, seeks to provide one of these Christian communities, that of evangelical Baptists, with reasons and resources for remembering the past. The editors are deeply convinced that Baptist history contains rich resources of theological reflection, praxis and spirituality that can help Baptists, as well as other Christians, live more Christianly in the present. The monographs in this series will therefore aim at illuminating various aspects of the Baptist tradition and in the process provide Baptists with a usable past.

Waiting on the Spirit of Promise

The Life and Theology of Suffering
of Abraham Cheare

Brian L. Hanson

with Michael A. G. Haykin

◦PICKWICK *Publications* • Eugene, Oregon

WAITING ON THE SPIRIT OF PROMISE
The Life and Theology of Suffering of Abraham Cheare

Monographs in Baptist History 1

Copyright © 2014 Brian L. Hanson and Michael A. G. Haykin. All rights reserved. Except for brief quotations in critical publications or reviews, no part of this book may be reproduced in any manner without prior written permission from the publisher. Write: Permissions, Wipf and Stock Publishers, 199 W. 8th Ave., Suite 3, Eugene, OR 97401.

Pickwick Publications
An Imprint of Wipf and Stock Publishers
199 W. 8th Ave., Suite 3
Eugene, OR 97401

www.wipfandstock.com

ISBN 13: 978-1-62564-237-0

Cataloging-in-Publication data:

Hanson, Brian L.

    Waiting on the spirit of promise : the life and theology of suffering of Abraham Cheare / Brian L. Hanson and Michael A. G. Haykin.

    xii + 104 p. ; 23 cm. —Includes bibliographical references.

    Monographs in Baptist History 1

    ISBN 13: 978-1-62564-237-0

    1. Cheare, Abraham, –1668. 2. Suffering—Religious aspects—Christianity—History of doctrines—17th century. 3. Baptists—Biography. I. Haykin, Michael A. G. II. Title. III. Series.

BT732.7 H23 2014

Manufactured in the U.S.A.

Permission to use image: © The British Library Board. (A true narration of the ... late seige of Plymouth, from the fifteenth day of September 1643, untill the twenty fift of December ... with an exact Map and Description of the Town and Fortifications, etc., London: L.N., for F. Eglesfeild, 1644.)

Contents

Introduction | ix

1. "Sweet for Jesus' Sake": The Life of Abraham Cheare | 1

2. "Lift up Our Voice Like a Trumpet":
   Cheare's Ministry in the 1650s | 11

3. "Waiting on the Spirit of Promise":
   Abraham Cheare in Prison in the 1660s | 25

4. A Letter of Abraham Cheare on Baptism, c. 1648–1658 | 41

5. Abraham Cheare, *Sighs for Sion* | 47

6. Abraham Cheare, *A Looking-Glass* | 61

7. Abraham Cheare, *Words in Season* | 83

   Letters | 89

   Bibliography | 101

"When I am gone, speak moderately of me I beseech you; but if anything hath been seen in me worth learning, let it be offered with much humility; or rather I think, let my works praise me in the gate."

ABRAHAM CHEARE

"Abraham Cheare deserves to be ranked among the Christian heroes of Devonshire."

G. HOLDEN PIKE

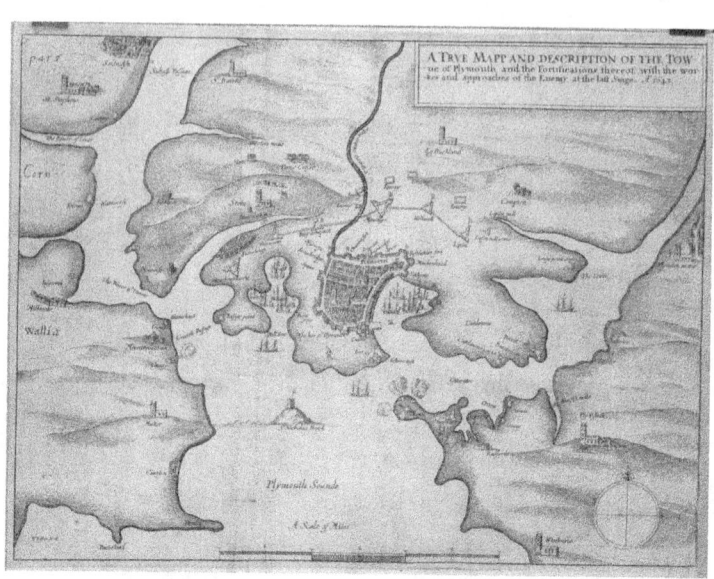

Introduction

THE HISTORY OF THE Baptists' reception of their own past is a fascinating one in its own right. Most of the Baptist works of the seventeenth century were never reprinted and consequently a significant amount of their thought was obscure to their eighteenth-century heirs. To be sure, there was a certain amount of reflection on the past by eighteenth-century authors like Thomas Crosby (1683–c. 1751) and Joseph Ivimey (1773–1834), both of whom wrote important histories of the English Baptists. But it was the Victorian Baptists who really began to delve into Baptist history and that for a variety of reasons. First, the Victorians in general were fascinated by the past—a fascination that is quite foreign to the modern mindset. Then, in England the exploration of Baptist history was linked to the realization in the 1850s of the strength of the Nonconformist cause and became a vehicle to express Baptist pride. In America, on the other hand, Baptist interest in the past was used by many to prove (or disprove) the theology of Landmarkism and to counteract Campbellism. Then came the twentieth century, which was probably the worst of all centuries for remembering the past. After World War I the ambience in the West was increasingly one in which the past was seen as old lumber to be discarded to make way for new perspectives, in the very same way that Victorian Gothic buildings were being leveled to make way for Art Deco and postmodernist structures. The past fifty years, though, have witnessed a renaissance of interest in the Puritans, both in regard to academic scholarship and popular literature, but this renaissance seems to have bypassed the Baptists. Nearly all of the Puritan figures who are being studied or read are either Presbyterians or Congregationalists. With the exception of the celebrated John Bunyan (1628–1688), rediscovered to a great extent by the Victorians, and to a lesser degree, Hanserd Knollys (1599–1691), William Kiffin (1616–1701) and Benjamin Keach (1640–1704), the Baptists of the seventeenth century have been largely forgotten. Thankfully this is changing, however, as Baptist scholars are rediscovering their forebears. And among these forebears is the subject of this small book, Abraham Cheare (1626–1668).

Why should an early twenty-first-century Christian take the time to learn about Abraham Cheare and read the portions of his writings contained in this small book? Well, first of all, suffering in prison for religious beliefs, as he did for eight years until it killed him, is not foreign to the modern world. Around the world, there are numerous contexts where religious toleration is all but non-existent and men and woman have to seriously count the cost if they wish to be public about their convictions. Even in the west an increasingly intolerant cultural elite are targeting the church and seeking to muzzle Christian witness. Here then, Cheare can help us enormously, for Cheare was a Puritan and after 1660, when the Anglican state church sought to extirpate Puritanism, Cheare and many others knew firsthand what it was to suffer for Christ's sake. His example and writings in this regard are tremendously helpful in forging a theology of suffering for Christians undergoing the same today.

Then, Cheare, above all things, sought to be guided by the Scriptures, not simply when it came to church polity but in all of his life. His life and writings exemplify what "being biblical" looks like. In this regard, then, he is a quintessential Puritan, for Puritanism was above all things a movement that sought to be Word-centered. Modern-day Christians would not cross every "t" and dot every "i" the way Cheare does; but his passion to be found living in accord with the Scriptures is certainly worthy of imitation. There is also a transparency about Cheare that is very refreshing: witness his account of the healing of a Captain Langdon and his hesitancy to baptize him in his letter that is found in chapter 4.

And simply reading the past for its own sake is important, for there we see God at work in the hurly-burly of life. To quote Richard Baxter (1615–1691), the Puritan contemporary of Cheare who also suffered for the sake of the gospel: "[T]he writing of church-history is the duty of all ages, because God's works are to be known, as well as his Word . . . He that knoweth not what state the church and world is in, and hath been in, in former ages, and what God hath been doing in the world, and how error and sin have been resisting him, and with what success, doth want much to the completing of his knowledge."[1] When the name of Abraham Cheare was recently mentioned to a close friend who is no stranger to the history of Christianity, he admitted he had never heard of Cheare and thought a study

---

1. Baxter, *The Life of Faith*, 364.

of his life might be somewhat "esoteric." Well, here is his life, some aspects of his theology, and especially his thinking about what it means to suffer for the sake of Christ: you, the reader, can judge whether the relative obscurity of this man and his thought lessens his importance as a witness (*martys*) for the Gospel of the Lord Jesus Christ.

Note: In our citations from Cheare's writings, we have modernized archaic spellings and we've brought biblical citations into accord with the modern use of Arabic numerals.

1

"Sweet for Jesus' Sake": The Life of Abraham Cheare

SEVERAL MONTHS BEFORE HIS premature death at the age of forty-one, Abraham Cheare (1626–1668) and his imprisoned friends received an unexpected gift of provisions that brightened their spirits. Though the "costly present" was given anonymously, Cheare and his friends were touched by those "whose hearts have made them willing, under the bounteous influences of the God of Israel, to comfort the hearts of the unworthy prisoners of the Lord in Plymouth Island."[1] They expressed their gratitude in a letter penned by Cheare for their givers' "holy liberality" and "expression of your sympathy."[2] In this letter, Cheare took the opportunity to inscribe a pastoral prayer for these benevolent saints. He prayed that they would obtain even "greater advances toward newness of heart," "greater approaches in a way of heavenliness and nearness to the Lord," and "right waitings for, and waitings on the Spirit of promise."[3] This small incident aptly illustrates Cheare's ability to draw rich spiritual applications from events in his life of suffering, a recurring practice throughout his life and evidence of his fervent piety.

As noted in the Introduction, English Baptist ministers of the seventeenth century have largely been overlooked in historical research. Yet from this period came men who exemplified a deep piety amidst intense suffering. Such a man was Abraham Cheare, a Baptist minister who labored in the middle part of the seventeenth century.[4] About half of Cheare's life as a

---

1. Cheare, *Words in Season*, 287.
2. Ibid., 288, 291.
3. Ibid., 291–92.
4. Various spellings of his name can be found, including Cheere, Chare, Chere, and Chaire. "Cheare" is by far the most common.

pastor entailed bitter suffering, in which he experienced the consequences of refusing to yield to those who would silence his preaching. Yet despite this fire of suffering, Cheare's life exuded a warm piety, which is still accessible in his extant writings. His writings are permeated by a sweetness that can yield an enriching experience for fellow pilgrims of a later generation. Close scrutiny and reflection on Cheare's life as found in his works provide a model on how to suffer well, embracing "the presence of a gracious God ... [that] makes the bitter of the rod, be sweet for Jesus' sake."[5]

The Early Particular Baptists

The formation of the very first Particular Baptist church in Wapping, London, around 1638, when John Spilsbury (1593–1668) led a body of believers out of the Jacob-Lathrop-Jessey church, paved the way for a number of Particular Baptist churches to be established across the British Isles in a relatively brief span of time. The Jacob-Lathrop-Jessey church, established in 1616 by Henry Jacob, thus became the fountain-head of the Particular Baptist heritage. The ecclesiological position of the Jacob-Lathrop-Jessey Church was one of association and cooperation with other Puritan churches, regardless of their ties to the Church of England. While other Separatists felt that partnership with any Puritan church that remained within the Church of England was to disobey biblical commands to separate, the leadership of the Jacob-Lathrop-Jessey Church felt that it was indeed right to continue fellowship with these Puritan churches because they were true churches. It was from within this circle that Spilsbury led a group out in order to establish a church in Wapping after he and those who went with him became convinced that paedobaptism was unbiblical.

By the mid-1640s, there were seven Particular Baptist churches in London. And sixteen years later that number had blossomed to 130 in the British Isles.[6] It is amazing that the British Civil Wars (1642–1651), though devastating to the country, did not disrupt the early growth of the Particular Baptists. Due to the fact that the Particular Baptist churches were the target of criticism and false accusations, Particular Baptist leaders drew up a doctrinal statement of fifty-three articles for the purpose of clarifying their doctrinal position. This *First London Confession of Faith* of 1644, published

---

5. Cheare and Jessey, *A Looking-Glass for Children*, 41.
6. Haykin, *Kiffin, Knollys and Keach*, 40.

two years later in a second edition, was drafted by Spilsbury, William Kiffin (1616–1701), and Samuel Richardson (1602–1658).[7] The hallmark of early Particular Baptist doctrine, the *Confession* played a significant role in the formation of Baptist doctrine and practice. While this work was intended to be apologetic in nature, since the Particular Baptists had been severely attacked by scathing charges from their opponents concerning doctrine and behavior, it also set the doctrinal parameters for the Baptist movement.

The first set of charges from the critics concerned Particular Baptist soteriology, namely, that they believed in free will, falling from grace, and original sin. Clearly, these critics had mistaken them for the General Baptists, who were Arminian, for Articles V, XXII, and XXIII attested to these Baptists' conviction with regard to God's sovereignty, perseverance of the saints, and original sin.[8] Second, it was believed that the Particular Baptists were revolutionaries and rabble-rousers, akin to some of the sixteenth-century Anabaptists on the European continent. The Anabaptists had garnered a reputation for fanaticism and violence due to the Münster incident of 1535 when Anabaptists seized the town and governed it with violence and as a theocracy. This was not the kind of image the English Baptists of the seventeenth century desired to have emblazoned on people's memories regarding themselves.[9] The authors of the *Confession* responded to this charge by clearly disassociating themselves from the contumacious tendencies of some of the Continental Anabaptists. The third charge was also serious and involved issues of morality. Opponents accused the Particular Baptists of sexual immorality and indecency in the act of baptism including being "stark naked, not only when they flock in great multitudes, men and women together, to their Jordans to be dipped; but also upon other occasions, when the season permits."[10] Again, this charge was shown to be groundless. In codifying Particular Baptist doctrine and practice, the *Confession* was therefore in part an attempt to demonstrate these

7. Ibid., 33

8. Ibid.

9. As late as 1761, the Münster incident was still being associated with the Baptists. John Martin (1741–1820), a High Calvinist minister in London, in *Some Account of the Life and Writings of the Rev. John Martin*, 48–50, admitted that the "frightful tales" of the infamous revolt was a hindrance to his conversion to Baptist doctrine. His memoir gives further credence to the fact that the English Baptists did not see themselves originating from the Anabaptists and their "wild and extravagant notions," from which they sought to distance themselves.

10. A charge made by Daniel Featley (1582–1645), cited by Haykin, *Kiffin, Knollys and Keach*, 34.

false accusations "as notoriously untrue" and to quell the brouhaha that had ensued about the presence of their congregations in the city.[11] It is in this turbulent era for the Particular Baptists that the ministry of Abraham Cheare needs to be placed.

Early Life and Ministry

Born in Plymouth "of mean yet honest parentage," Abraham Cheare was baptized as an infant on 28 May 1626.[12] The entries in the record books of St. Andrew's Church indicate that his parents, John Cheare and Joane Norbroncke, were married on 18 January 1617 at St. Andrew's Church in Plymouth.[13] The younger Cheare had four older siblings: Elizabeth, Joane, John, and John.[14] He was raised by his parents "in the poor yet honest trade of a fuller," his father also being a fuller.[15] Not much is known of his parents, other than the mention of his father leasing some tucking mills in Plymouth, one of which was the Western Fulling Mill.[16] Cheare's youth remains obscure, though it is known that he never received a university education, having been confined to Plymouth to work with his father.[17] Nathan Brookes, the publisher of one of his books, noted that his parents were also believers who took care to nurture their son in God's ways.[18] Cheare rarely left Plymouth with the exception of some brief journeys and his imprisonment.[19] There is no indication that Cheare ever married. Cheare did have some nieces and nephews, as at least one of his two sisters was married.[20]

11. *London Baptist Confession of Faith*, http://www.spurgeon.org/~phil/creeds/bc1644.htm.

12. Nicholson, *A History of the Baptist Church Now Meeting in George Street Chapel, Plymouth from 1620*, 17; Foster, "Early Baptist Writers of Verse," 95. Foster mistakenly identifies this date as Cheare's actual birth date.

13. Nicholson, *History*, 17. We are indebted to Mr. Thomas Maddock of Plymouth who graciously provided us with a copy of the original entry from the church record books in the Plymouth and West Devon Records Office, Plymouth.

14. Nicholson, *History*, 17. The third child, John, was buried on 17 December 1622 shortly before his second birthday. The cause of death is unknown.

15. Nicholson, *History*, 16.

16. Ibid.

17. Cheare, "Post-script" to his *Words in Season*, 293.

18. Cheare, "The Publisher to the Reader" in *Words in Season*, [6].

19. Cheare, "Post-script" to his *Words in Season*, 293.

20. Cheare, *Words in Season*, 186.

During the tense times of the British Civil Wars, Plymouth, with its many formidable forts, became the object of a number of unsuccessful sieges and blockades due to its staunch support of the Parliamentarian cause. Charles I (r.1625–1649) arrived at Plymouth with his Royalist troops in 1644 and established his headquarters nearby.[21] Cheare never enlisted in the Parliamentarian army, though he did serve for a period of time in the local militia of Plymouth.[22] He also served as a military chaplain against his will for just a few weeks and was able to obtain a discharge from that role.[23] Around 1648, Cheare was baptized as a believer and "joined himself in an holy covenant, to walk in all the ordinances of the Lord blameless, to the best of his light and power, in fellowship with a poor and despised people."[24] This "poor and despised people" with whom he entered into fellowship was the Calvinistic Baptist church in Plymouth.[25] That same year he was called to minister to this church and was ordained.[26] One hundred and fifty members affixed their signatures to the church record books in approval of their new minister.[27]

Imprisonment and Exile

Oliver Cromwell's death in 1658 terminated the short-lived Commonwealth, shattering the dreams of Nonconformist toleration and plunging England again into political turmoil. The Restoration of the Stuart monarchy with the ascension of Charles II (r.1660–1685) to the throne in 1660 began an era of severe persecution for the Nonconformists and their ministers. The

---

21. Nicholson, *History*, 14.
22. Cheare, "Post-script" to his *Words in Season*, 293.
23. Ibid., 294.
24. Ibid.
25. Nicholson, *History*, 14; see a photo of George Street Baptist Chapel, Plymouth at http://www.flickr.com/photos/plymouthhistory/6003709582/. The church was established in 1620 according to the church record books, though nothing else is known regarding its formation or any of Cheare's predecessors, Cheare being the first recorded minister. The church later became George Street Baptist Church. The church was bombed by the Nazi *Luftwaffe* during the Blitz of Plymouth on 21 March 1941. The life of the church continues in the present day at Catherine Street Baptist Church in Plymouth City Centre. We are indebted to Rev. Veronica Campbell, present minister of the church, for confirming these details.
26. Nicholson, *History*, 15.
27. Ibid.

purpose of this persecution was to restore the status of the state church as the only religious body of the land and so maintain its supremacy in all religious affairs of the nation. This situation was exacerbated by Thomas Venner (d.1661), a minister of the Swan Alley congregation in London, who launched a public rebellion in 1661, prompting the monarchy to suppress all Nonconformists.[28] Venner belonged to the Fifth Monarchy movement, which, on the basis of a distinct reading of Daniel 2, believed that Jesus was about to return to establish his millennial kingdom and that its coming could be hastened by military action. Though definitely not of this persuasion, Cheare was arrested in 1661 for "encouraging religious assemblies" and imprisoned for three months in Exeter.[29] Charles II's coronation on 23 April 1661 brought a temporary respite to nonconformist ministers, including Cheare, who were released from their imprisonment. It was not long, however, until Puritanism within the Church of England was dealt a fatal blow with the passing of the Act of Uniformity on 19 May 1662 and its subsequent execution on 24 August 1662, St. Bartholomew's Day, leading to the Great Ejection of upwards of two thousand ministers who refused to give "unfeigned assent and consent to all and everything contained and prescribed in and by . . . the Book of Common Prayer."[30]

Cheare refused to subscribe to the provisions of the Act, including taking the Oath of Allegiance and was imprisoned again in 1662 for holding "unlawful assemblies" and for refusing "to conform to the laws of the Established Church."[31] His imprisonment in the Exeter jail would last for three grueling years in which he suffered "under very hard circumstances, enduring many inhumanities from merciless goalers."[32] In the meantime, Cheare's congregation suffered bitterly at the hands of the Plymouth au-

---

28. For details of Venner's Rebellion including his trial and death sentence, see *The last Speech and Prayer with other Passages of Thomas Venner*. For Venner's thinking, see Bernard Capp, "A Door of Hope Re-opened," 16–30. Interestingly enough, Cheare did associate with a Fifth Monarchist, Thomas Glasse (d. 1666), who co-signed Cheare's *Sighs for Sion* and for whom Cheare wrote a lengthy elegy at the time of his death entitled "A Mourner's Mite" (*Looking-Glass*, 89–93). However, there is no evidence at all that Cheare accepted the beliefs or revolutionary practices of the Fifth Monarchy movement.

29. Ivimey, *A History of English Baptists*, 2:104.

30. Cited in White, *The English Baptists of the Seventeenth Century*, 103. For details of the Act of Uniformity and its consequences upon unlicensed preachers, see F. A. [pseud.], *A Letter from a Gentleman in Grayes-Inn, to a Justice of the Peace in the Countrey*.

31. Cited in Nicholson, *Authentic Records Relating to the Christian Church*, 16.

32. Cheare, *Words in Season*, 175.

thorities in 1662–1663, with many congregants being imprisoned alongside Cheare.[33] The mayor of Plymouth in these years was William Jennens (1614–c.1687), who was a zealot when it came to the suppression of Nonconformity and Cheare and his fellow Baptists could expect no mercy under his regime.[34] Though permanently hindered from ministering to his congregation, Cheare's affection for and interest in his people remained unabated. In fact, on his deathbed he admitted that "he had oft, since his sickness, on his bed, begg'd of God, that the Lord the God of the spirits of all flesh, would send a man over that church."[35]

Though his pulpit and on-site pastoral ministry were permanently muzzled, Cheare continued his ministry to his congregation and friends by drafting correspondence to them and composing poetry in his prison cell. These prison writings were compiled posthumously in *Words in Season* and *A Looking-Glass For Children*. What is striking about these writings is their transparency and the acute anguish that Cheare did not hesitate to express. During his time in prison, he was given a couple of opportunities to take the Oath of Allegiance, which would have restored him back to his pulpit in Plymouth, but he rejected these offers.[36] In 1663 at the Midsummer Sessions, Cheare was charged with praemunire—a travesty of the law—and as a result, all of his property was confiscated and he was once again subject to imprisonment.[37] Cheare was permitted to leave his cell in August 1665 and went to Plymouth in order to stay with one of his sisters.[38] His enemies, eager to have him banished for good, reported him to the local magistrates who re-arrested him only a month after his release. He was confined in the Guildhall at Plymouth for the month of September.[39] And on 27 September

---

33. Nicholson, *History*, 43; Rippon, *The Baptist Annual Register*, 3:276–85. The church at Plymouth endured intense persecution from local authorities for over twenty years. The church was without a minister until 30 November 1687 when they called Robert Brown (d. 1688) to be their pastor. The church membership had dwindled to sixty-six by that time. For details on this period of the church's history, see Nicholson, *History*, 73–75.

34. Gill, *Plymouth*, 162–63.

35. Cheare, *Words in Season*, 176.

36. Foster, "Early Baptist Writers of Verse," 98. On Cheare's own views of accepting offers of deliverance, see *Words in Season*, 56–63. Cheare stated that when believers receive an unconditional offer of deliverance that does not violate the Scriptures, it is "a very high duty incumbent" on them to accept such an offer.

37. Foster, "Early Baptist Writers of Verse," 98.

38. Rippon, *Baptist Annual Register*, 3:276.

39. For a description of the squalid conditions and dimensions of the Guildhall in

1665, Cheare was transported to exile for life on Drake's Island just off the coast in Plymouth Sound.[40]

Within several days of his arrival on the Island, he contracted a "violent sickness" that took such a toll on his body that his health was permanently shattered.[41] For the next two and a half years he was alone in his cell, suffering both physically and emotionally, yet composing voluminously. As he confessed: "the salt sharp air is manifestly ruinous to my health, exposing me (more than ever I was in my life) to daily distempers."[42] In the main, though, those years were uneventful with the exception of "threatened transportation" to one of England's newly acquired islands in the West Indies in 1666.[43]

This "threatened transportation" had its roots in the Conventicle Act of 1664, which was designed to regulate worship and curb ongoing meetings by Nonconformists.[44] One of the penalties of violating the provisions of the Act was seven years of exile to the West Indies to join African slaves in working on the sugar plantations. These years saw the rise of the sugar trade, with sugar becoming increasingly a staple commodity in England. More workers were needed to assist the African slaves, and sending the recalcitrant Nonconformists was far less expensive than sailing to West Africa to acquire more slaves. No doubt, this was unnerving to Cheare and other Nonconformists, because at least in prison they were able to derive solace from writing letters to their family and friends. In the West Indies, that would no longer be possible. The possibility of transportation appears to have caused much angst for Cheare. The threat never materialized, how-

---

Plymouth, see Nicholson, *History*, 49–50.

40. For information on Drake's Island, see "Fortifications: 1600–1699" from Drake's Island Plymouth website: http://www.drakesislandplymouth.co.uk/#/fortifications/4547113160. Drake's Island, known as St. Nicholas Island at the time, had been used as a Parliamentarian fort to defend Plymouth from Royalist attack during the English Civil War. It was transformed into a prison in 1661 for Nonconformists and political opponents of the Crown. Cheare is recorded as the last prisoner of Drake's Island. Thereafter, the island resumed its former status as a military fort. See Nicholson, *History*, 51.

Cheare was not the only minister from Plymouth imprisoned on Drake's Island. George Hughes (1603–1667), the Puritan vicar of St. Andrew's Church, and his lecturer, Thomas Martyn, were also prisoners.

41. Cheare, *Words in Season*, 175.

42. Ibid., 265.

43. Ibid., 265; Nicholson, *History*, 54.

44. For information on the Conventicle Act, see White, *English Baptists of the Seventeenth Century*, 105–7, 109–13; Spence, *The Church of England*, 170.

ever, for reasons that are not known, but judging from Cheare's other letters around this period, his health was so poor that he would have been hardly fit to labor in West Indian sugar cane fields. Cheare's health continued to deteriorate and his sister and certain friends were permitted to attend to him in his island cell during his final days.[45] He passed away peacefully from this life on 5 March 1668 at the age of forty-one.[46]

Conclusion

Though brief, his life appeared to be one of fervent piety, shaped especially by his sufferings. His robust determination to submit to adverse circumstances in spite of separation from his congregation and the failure of his health was remarkable. To "kiss the rod" of suffering revealed a courageous and humble spirit, not one merely resigned to fate, but one driven by faith to "embrace the sentence of a gibbet, a stake, a rack, an ax, an halter, a transportation into exile" if there is no possible way of escape.[47] It was an act of a "poor captive" to "abandon other lords [and] to Jesus bow," because, in the end, he was bound not to Parliament, but to the "most glorious Sovereign" to whom he vowed, "here am I, let him do with me what seemeth good in his sight."[48]

---

45. Cheare, *Words in Season*, 175–217. Cheare's sister was unidentified in his final words. She was apparently married with children. She evidently broke down in tears several times in grief to see Cheare in his dying state. At one occasion there were five others in the cell with him: a fellow believer, a maid, a nurse, a friend, and his own sister.

46. Ibid., 217; Nicholson, *History*, 59; Foster, "Early Baptist Writers of Verse," 95. Brookes, in *Words in Season*, records "the 5th day of the first Month, 1668." Up to 1752, the calendar year in England began in March. Foster states that his death was "5 March, 1667-8." The year was certainly not 1667, because Cheare composed some letters in the latter part of 1667.

47. Cheare, *Words in Season*, 101.

48. Cheare, *Looking-Glass*, 87–88; idem, *Words in Season*, 47.

2

"Lift up Our Voice Like a Trumpet": Cheare's Ministry in the 1650s

THE PARTICULAR BAPTISTS WERE initially thrilled with the appointment of Oliver Cromwell (1599–1658) as Lord Protector of England in 1653, due to the fact that his sympathies were with them. At the time, the future appeared promising for the Baptists. As already noted, during the era of the Commonwealth the Particular Baptist churches as a denominational body experienced significant growth; and the Baptist work at Plymouth under Cheare's able leadership likewise flourished during this period. In fact, the church so grew in its attendance that another building was needed to accommodate the burgeoning numbers. In 1651 the church purchased some land in the Pig Market district and established a new house for worship.[1]

Active in the Western Association

Not only was this a time of prosperity for the individual Baptist churches of England, but it was also a period in which associations of these churches were initiated within set geographical bounds across the Commonwealth. These associations were born from a deep-seated conviction that individual churches were not merely to exist and function as disparate entities. This conviction was first articulated in the *First London Confession of Faith* of 1644: "Although the particular congregations be distinct and several bodies, every one a compact and knit city in itself: yet are they all to walk by one and the same rule, and by all means convenient to have the counsel and

---

1. Nicholson, *A History of the Baptist Church*, 15; Rippon, *The Baptist Annual Register*, 3:274.

help one of another in all needful affairs of the church, as members of one body in the common faith under Christ their only head."[2]

The Western Association, of which Cheare's church was an early member, was founded in 1653. At that time it was specified that this association existed so that "the Gospel may have a free course and be glorified everywhere, to the gathering in all the elect to the faith and obedience of Christ and to that end that much of the Spirit may be given to the churches to the preparing and thrusting forth fit labourers not only among the Gentiles but also, if it be His pleasure to use us, among the house of Abraham His friend."[3] Cheare took an active role in the Western Association. For example, though he remained in Plymouth, Cheare was instrumental in the planting of a Particular Baptist church in Cornwall around 1655. He engaged in correspondence with Colonel Robert Bennet (1605–1683), who was a member of the House of Commons in 1653 and 1654, concerning the founding of this church, and recommended that the London Baptist pastor Hanserd Knollys (1599–1691) be involved in it. He also encouraged Bennet to contact William Kiffin.[4] The following year Cheare sent at least one delegate from his church to attend the Association meeting in Exeter on 6 August 1656.[5] The missionary focus evident in the quote above was especially discussed during this meeting in 1656. The delegates resolved to "more sensibly sympathize with the state and condition of the whole Zion of God by being delivered from the spirit of the world and those carnal interests of earth and men wherein so many mind their own things in the neglect of Christ and one another."[6] These ministers went so far as to publish a circular letter to the Association churches that pled with them to be committed to cross-cultural missions. In the words of the letter: "It much concerneth us to be up and doing, to put our hands to the work, not only

---

2. *First London Confession of Faith* 47 in Lumpkin, *Baptist Confessions of Faith*, 168–69.

3. Cited in Nicholson, *History*, 25.

4. Howson, *Erroneous and Schismatical Opinions*, 68 n. 56; White, "Early Baptist Letters (I)," 148 n. 6; Bennet, "Guide to the Papers of Robert Bennet, 1603-1678," see the "Collection Details" section at http://titania.folger.edu/findingaids/dfobennet.xml. Bennet was originally from Cornwall and served in the Parliamentarian army during the Civil War. He was a man of significant influence in Cornwall, representing it in the Parliament of the Saints during the Interregnum.

5. Nicholson, *History*, 25.

6. Cited in Nicholson, *History*, 25.

in this nation but also to pray that it may be carried on in other parts of the world as the Lord may open up a way."[7]

In May of 1658, Cheare himself attended a pivotal meeting of the Western Association in Dorchester. Several prominent Fifth Monarchists including John Carew (1622–1660) were in attendance at the gathering, attempting to persuade the Association ministers to forge a partnership with them for the purpose of launching an armed attack on the government. Cheare along with William Kiffin denounced their plot and the proposal was vehemently condemned *in toto* by the Association.[8]

It needs noting that not only did Cheare provide leadership among the churches of the Western Association, but he also made contributions to the Midland Association. At Devizes in Wiltshire on 9 July 1657, Cheare and William Kiffin met with four other ministers of the Midland Association to discuss items including state stipends for ministers and submission to the government.[9] And in May of that same year, Cheare issued an appeal to this Association for financial support for destitute ministers in the West Country. His request was accepted, and the Particular Baptist leaders in London took the initiative in passing a resolution to create a fund in the Midland Association's budget for the "maintenance of a gospel ministry abroad in the countries."[10]

Sighs for Sion

Cheare's love for the church was not only demonstrated by his active involvement in the planting of Particular Baptist churches, but also by the writing of two crucial tracts, the first one promoting the unity of these churches and the second defending their doctrinal purity. The first treatise composed by Cheare during these formative years of church associations, *Sighs for Sion*, was the work chiefly of Cheare and it was co-signed by four other Particular Baptist leaders, Henry Forty (1625–1692),[11] John

---

7. Cited in Nicholson, *History*, 26.

8. Woolrych, *Britain in Revolution: 1625–1660*, 690.

9. White, "The Organisation of the Particular Baptists, 1644–1660," 12. White's article details the founding and activities of the Midland Association.

10. Cited in ibid.

11. For more on Henry Forty see, Ivimey, *A History of English Baptists*, 2:66–68; Nuttall, "Abingdon Revisited, 1656–1675," 96–103. Forty, a signatory of the 1651 edition of the *First London Confession*, was initially a member of the Jacob-Lathrop-Jessey Church.

Pendarves (1622–1656),[12] Thomas Glasse (d.1666),[13] and Robert Steed (d.1703?).[14] This tract, published in 1656, was addressed to Particular Baptist churches for the purpose of "awakening them that are at ease, and pressing and encouraging all the upright in heart" for the welfare of "Sion," Christ's church.[15] In this work Cheare appealed for unity within the context of heightened squabbles over eschatological views, specifically those endorsed by the Fifth Monarchists.[16]

Cheare opened the tract with a riveting confession by the ministers for possessing a "narrowness of our own spirits" and "a self-seeking and self-pleasing spirit."[17] He admitted that their own "private interest of peace and comfort is more sensibly wrapped up" in themselves.[18] The ministers of the Particular Baptist churches were not the only ones guilty of this self-centered spirit, he contended, but it extended to the churches themselves. This spirit was damaging, disruptive, and deadening to the health of the churches. Provincialism and excessive autonomy among the churches was ultimately pathetic and rooted in pride. In Cheare's words: "Men are sleeping, lying down, loving to slumber in every corner, saying, It is not nigh; let us build houses . . . And is not pride, and fullness of bread companions

---

By the time of his signing the Preface of *Sighs For Sion*, he was pastor of a church in Devonshire. He was imprisoned in Exeter for twelve years for his Baptist convictions. Upon his release in 1672, he returned to London to pastor the church where he originated from, the Jacob-Lathrop-Jessey Church. In 1675, Forty became the pastor of Abingdon Baptist Church, which John Pendarves had founded and pastored, until his death in 1692.

12. For more on John Pendarves, see Ivimey, *History of English Baptists*, 2:62–64; "History of Abingdon Baptist Church" (http://www.abingdonbaptist.org.uk/abc6_023.htm). Shortly after his graduation from Exeter College, Oxford in 1642, Pendarves began his preaching ministry as an itinerant evangelist. He then assumed a position as the vicar of St. Helen's Church in Abingdon until 1647. After he became convinced of Baptist principles, he became the founding minister of the Abingdon Baptist Church and served there from 1649 to his death in 1656.

13. For more on Thomas Glasse, see Capp, *The Fifth Monarchy Men*, 203–5; Nuttall, "Abingdon Revisited, 1656–1675," 96–103. An advocate of the Fifth Monarchy movement, Glasse was originally from Devon and eventually settled in London. He was minister of the Baptist church in Bovey-Tracey, Devon, when *Sighs for Sion* was written.

14. Cheare, *Sighs for Sion*.

15. Ibid., title page. See below, p. 48.

16. For the beliefs of the Fifth Monarchists, see Capp, *The Fifth Monarchy Men*; and Anderson, "A Fifth Monarchist Appeal." For the relationship between Fifth Monarchism and the Particular Baptists, see White, "John Pendarves."

17. Cheare, *Sighs for Sion*, 5. See below, p. 50.

18. Ibid. See below, p. 50.

to this abundant idleness, through which the building decayeth?"[19] The churches, in Cheare's estimation, were in desperate straits and on the brink of unmitigated disaster. As he said, speaking with regard to them in universal tones: "A disappointment hath befallen many of her [i.e. the church's] hopeful expectations, because her transgressions are many: reproach hath befallen her at the hands of professors; and the enemies that know not the Lord, blaspheme."[20]

Foundational to Cheare's confession and subsequent appeal was an exalted view of the universal church. Cheare provided a sharp contrast between the church's value and its actual deplorable state in his day. The church was Christ's body and for it He sacrificed Himself. Christ as the Head of His church elected His people from every nation so that they were now "God's called and faithful people ... the peculiar people of God upon the face of the whole earth."[21] Furthermore, Christ viewed the church as "a blessed bride ... this blessed people, this Sion, God's glorious building, and workmanship in Christ."[22] By arguing for the value and special identity of the universal church, Cheare was communicating to the English Baptist churches the necessity of striving for unity and interdependence within their own network of Particular Baptists. It was vital, therefore, that the English Baptist churches abandon their "self-seeking spirit" and individual interests and arouse their sympathies for the broader church.

By what method and means was unity to be achieved among the Particular Baptist churches across England? Cheare urged the churches not to be encumbered with tertiary matters such as millenarianism—the Fifth Monarchists were in view here clearly—but rather to pursue the greatest cause of the church, "the advancement of that name, interest, and glory of God, that should be upon our hearts, to have made manifest in all the earth, from the rising of the sun, and from the west."[23] He exhorted them to affirm the church's inestimable value by being "suitably affected with an holy sympathy in her state, through that one Spirit that is in promise for all her children, that you may truly say, as souls whom faith and love have transported into her interests, All my springs are in thee [Ps 87:7]."[24] It was paramount,

19. Ibid., 14. See below, p. 57.
20. Ibid., 17. See below, p. 58.
21. Ibid., 7. See below, p. 52.
22. Ibid., 8. See below, p. 52. The terms "*bride*" and "*Sion*" are in capitals in the original. The change to italics retains the original emphasis.
23. Ibid., 5. See below, p. 50.
24. Ibid., 6. See below, p. 51.

he reasoned, that the churches put aside their "divers differences…touching the time, way and manner of God's effecting those great things" and embrace "the spirit of faith and love" as they with "one mind, give their power and strength to the Lamb."[25] Cheare's exhortation was strikingly similar to Article 34 of the *First London Confession of Faith* in which members of the universal church are "to lead their lives in his walled sheepfold, and watered garden, to have communion here with the Saints."[26] The evocative imagery about the church employed by the authors of the *Confession* designated it as a place of protection from external and internal turbulence.[27] Communion of the saints was a sacrosanct duty of those within the church. Consequently, sectarianism was to be shunned at all costs. Because it was so enervating to the health of the churches, separation over tertiary matters was not a viable option. As the *First London Confession* put it: "Thus being rightly gathered, established, and still proceeding in Christian communion, and obedience of the Gospel of Christ, none ought to separate for faults and corruptions, which may, and as long as the church consists of men subject to failings, will fall out and arise amongst them, even in true constituted churches, until they have in due order sought redress thereof."[28]

Drawing from the Old Testament, Cheare put forth David, Nehemiah, and Ezra as models for the churches to aspire to, for they "set their hearts and hands about the work of Sion."[29] While emulating these Old Testament saints and refraining from internal bickering over minor doctrinal matters were certainly essential, they were not sufficient in and of themselves to bring blessing, affirmed Cheare. What the churches ultimately needed was "a mighty spirit of faith and prayer."[30] It was through this "spirit of faith and prayer night and day" that God would extend His mercy to Sion, because "the Lord is delighted in the faithful fervent prayers of those who have sought him."[31] In a powerful exhortation Cheare urged the members of the Particular Baptist churches to reflect on what kind of congregations

---

25. Ibid., 10–11. See below, p. 54.

26. Lumpkin, *Baptist Confessions of Faith*, 166.

27. Haykin, *Kiffin, Knollys and Keach*, 36.

28. *London Baptist Confession of Faith* 46 in Lumpkin, *Baptist Confessions of Faith*, 168.

29. Cheare, *Sighs for Sion*, 12. See below, p. 55.

30. Ibid., 15. See below, p. 57.

31. Ibid., 16, 13. See below, pp. 58, 56.

they ought to be like. Were they the sort of people they should be, then, Cheare and his fellow authors wrote,

> the zeal of the Lord's house would eat us up, and love of it would crucify us more unto, and wean us from those interests of earth, and men, whereupon we have been apt to lean, and whereunto we have been deeply and dangerously engaged: causing us also to wait to be with Jesus, which is best of all; and in the mean time to pant, and thirst incessantly, for that holy Spirit of promise, that alone can present us with the ravishing glory of that expected day, and raise up our spirits to a sweet and suitable disposition, according to the will of God, to wait and act aright toward it.[32]

Cheare's exhortation to "pant and thirst incessantly, for that holy Spirit of promise" was a concern that stayed with him to the end of his days. More than once in his final work, his posthumously published *Words in Season*, he made reference to waiting for the Holy Spirit. For example, one of his final pieces of admonition to his Plymouth congregation, written on 22 November 1667, was for them "to press and pursue after . . . right waitings for, and waitings on the Spirit of promise, who is of power to quicken dry bones, raise dead witnesses, and do great things in and for us."[33] There was a realization embedded in this admonition that the hope of all that Cheare and his fellow Baptists had labored for ultimately lay in the power of the Holy Spirit. It was he who was needed to quicken dead sinners—an allusion to Ezekiel 37—and it was he who was needed to empower those he called to be his witnesses—and here Cheare alluded to Revelation 11:11.

Cheare closed *Sighs for Sion* by making a heartfelt appeal to his fellow ministers to labor indefatigably for the work of building Sion: "Dear hearts, let your faith be high, and your wrestlings without weariness; neither be ye in any measure discouraged, nor discouraging one another . . . do it, we pray you, as for his, and his people's sake, with all your might; not sparing to lay out your more worthy labours, for the carrying on of this work."[34] This "weighty work" was to be performed not only for the sake of the universal church, but ultimately for the "name and glory of God (which ought to be dearer to us than our lives)."[35]

32. Ibid., 18–19. See below, p. 60.
33. Cheare, *Words in Season*, 291, 292; see also 258–61.
34. Cheare, *Sighs for Sion*, 21. See below, pp. 60–61.
35. Ibid., 20–21. See below, p. 61. The phrase *"name and glory of God,"* is in capitals in the original. The change to italics retains the original emphasis.

A Plain Discovery

A treatise by Richard Bellamy, a member of only two years' standing in the Particular Baptist church in Tiverton, threatened to undermine the unity and doctrinal purity of the Particular Baptists that Cheare and others had articulated in *Sighs for Sion*. Entitled *The Leper Cleansed* (1658), Bellamy unleashed his fury upon the Particular Baptists after he had been excommunicated from his church for his refusal to repent of what had been deemed misconduct, which was specifically designated as "beneath civility, and much more beneath Christianity."[36] The misconduct centered on his relationship with his parents-in-law, to whom he had made requests vis-à-vis his marriage. When his parents-in-law did not acquiesce to these requests, Bellamy responded with rancor, calling his father-in-law an "old knave" and his mother-in-law "a serpent that lay in his [Bellamy's] bosom."[37] Even after two members of the church, one of whom actually witnessed the event, confronted and rebuked him, Bellamy refused to repent and denied that he had uttered such things. A few other members of the church urged him to reconsider his rash behavior, but it was to no avail as he maintained his "stubborn spirit."[38] The church, as a *pis aller*, assembled together and issued a public exhortation, calling him to repent of his sin, also threatening excommunication if unheeded. Bellamy refused to submit and broke fellowship with the church.

Bellamy's tract, a "caution [to] young ignorant Christians against the error of that way," was a scathing diatribe against the Particular Baptists for two primary reasons.[39] First, he rejected the Baptists' position on infant baptism, a practice that he argued was by "God's appointment."[40] Second, he took issue with the church in Tiverton for neglecting the spiritual disciplines, tolerating sermons lacking in conviction, and having a "deadness of spirit."[41] So biting was Bellamy's invective about the Particular Baptist churches in the rural West Country of England that it caused Cheare to lament, "The reproach of this, falls heavier upon us in the countries, than it

---

36. Cheare and Steed, *Plain Discovery*, 70–71.
37. Ibid., 70.
38. Ibid.
39. Bellamy, *The Leper Cleansed*, title page.
40. Ibid., 6; Cheare and Steed, *Plain Discovery*, 8.
41. Bellamy, *Leper Cleansed*, 27; Cheare and Steed, *Plain Discovery*, 75.

doth on them in that town, where the advantages of informing the enquirers, and clearing the accused, are at hand."[42]

Published the same year as Bellamy's treatise, *A Plain Discovery of the Unrighteousness Judge and False Accuser* was a detailed response by Abraham Cheare and Robert Steed to Bellamy's accusations.[43] Their purpose was one of "vindicating the churches of Christ . . . from such notorious slanders" and "to give men a warning at present against such artifices to deceive."[44] The indictments leveled at the Baptists along with Bellamy's vitriolic and inimical tone were serious. He called their ways "unchristian" and spoke of their "ways and wiles to deceive."[45] The Baptists, furthermore, were "cunning deceivers, lyers in wait, hypocrites, enemies to godliness, enemies to magistracy and ministry."[46] In order to "clear our selves from such an heap of slanders," Cheare and Steed set out to expose the "naked truth" by "giving forth the narrative with all exactness."[47] Their methodology in addressing Bellamy was "to follow our accuser step by step; wherein we repeat his words: and have willingly omitted nothing that deserves an answer."[48] Cheare and Steed organized the tract with an interchange of headings labeled "Accuser" and "Answer," quoting directly from Bellamy's *The Leper Cleansed* followed by their refutation of the accuser's allegations.

First, they addressed the issue of infant baptism by elucidating Baptist soteriology and ecclesiology. Their meticulous unpacking of theology was designed to defend Baptist doctrine and to repudiate the charge by Bellamy that Particular Baptist principles and practices were "loose."[49] Cheare and

42. Cheare and Steed, "To the Reader" in Cheare and Steed, *Plain Discovery*, [ii].

43. For more on Robert Steed, see Wilson, *History and Antiquities*, 2:571; "Original Letters," 23; Ivimey, *A History of English Baptists*, 3:361; Binmore, *The History of the Baptist Church, Dartmouth*. Steed was initially the minister of the Baptist church in Dartmouth. He later became Hanserd Knollys' assistant at Broken Wharf Church until Knollys' death in 1691, when he assumed the role of minister until his own death around 1703. He was one of the signatories of the *Second London Confession* of 1689. In addition, he had a significant role in the congregational singing controversy among the English Baptist churches. Ironically, he took the opposing side to Hanserd Knollys, who argued in favor of the congregational singing of psalms and hymns. See Howson, *Erroneous and Schismatical Opinions*, 76 n. 95.

44. Cheare and Steed, "To the Reader" in Cheare and Steed, *Plain Discovery*, [i].

45. Bellamy, *Leper Cleansed*, title page.

46. Cheare and Steed, *Plain Discovery*, 1.

47. Cheare and Steed, "To the Reader" in Cheare and Steed, *Plain Discovery*, [ii].

48. Ibid.

49. Bellamy, *Leper Cleansed*, 5; Cheare and Steed, *Plain Discovery*, 4–5.

Steed argued that the practice of paedobaptism had "no colour of warrant from the Word of God."[50] "There can be found no such appointment instituted by Christ, or any of his Apostles, for the baptizing of the children of believers."[51] There were no Scriptural grounds, they continued, for a church ordinance "to be practicable duly by a person in an unregenerate state."[52] Cheare and Steed responded to Bellamy's conclusion that Particular Baptist children "could have no hope of their children" because of their churches' position on baptism by affirming that hope of salvation was grounded in the gospel, not in the practice of baptism.[53] Baptism was reserved exclusively for those who made a public "profession of actual faith in the Son of God."[54] Faith and repentance, they averred, were the prerequisites of salvation and, hence, Christian baptism.[55] At this juncture, their argument and wording ran parallel with Article 39 of the *First London Confession of Faith*: "Baptism is an ordinance of the new Testament, given by Christ, to be dispensed only upon persons professing faith, or that are disciples, or taught, who upon a profession of faith, ought to be baptized."[56]

Inextricably linked to the issue of baptism was the covenant of grace, a covenant that Bellamy viewed as "stand[ing] now in force to the children of believers under the Gospel."[57] Cheare and Steed briefly traced the covenant of grace through the Old Testament from Genesis 3:15 to the writings of Isaiah, concluding that the covenant "hath passed under many great alterations and changes" that they called "administrations."[58] The first administration of the covenant of grace, they maintained, was the old covenant as given to Moses and the children of Israel. That covenant was appropriate and binding for that era, but was "then to be utterly cast out of the church."[59] Consequently, the covenant of grace in its original form was no longer in force. The final administration of the covenant of grace, the

---

50. Cheare and Steed, *Plain Discovery*, 27.

51. Ibid., 15.

52. Ibid., *Plain Discovery*, 27.

53. Bellamy, *Leper Cleansed*, 8; Cheare and Steed, *Plain Discovery*, 27–28.

54. Cheare and Steed, *Plain Discovery*, 13.

55. Ibid., *Plain Discovery*, 16.

56. Lumpkin, *Baptist Confessions of Faith*, 167.

57. Cheare and Steed, *Plain Discovery*, 7–8.

58. Ibid., *Plain Discovery*, 9.

59. Ibid., *Plain Discovery*, 11. The strength of the phrase "utterly cast out" here is striking. It bespeaks the seventeenth-century Baptist consciousness of the discontinuity between the old and new covenants.

new covenant, replaced the Old Testament form of the covenant of grace, eliminating the need for circumcision and the "birth-privilege" that accompanied the first administration. A profession of faith, not baptism, was now the obligatory prerequisite of the new covenant. Therefore, baptism was a sign of one professing faith and becoming a member of Christ's church. Not only was it a sign, they explained, but "the ordinance of baptism, is a part of the instituted worship of the Gospel, and all the force and authority that it hath upon the conscience in point of practice, is to be derived from the plain and express law and word of God, by which it is made an ordinance of the gospel: and that in point of practice must be the rule not to be swerved from."[60]

Second, Cheare and Steed refuted Bellamy's accusation that the Particular Baptists neglected corporate and personal piety. Bellamy indicted them for being "sleight in their thoughts of the Sabbath, and that they observed that day rather out of policy than out of conscience."[61] Cheare and Steed debunked this disparaging remark as "wormwood and gall," insisting that all Particular Baptists "do hold our selves bound to keep the first day of the week, called the Lord's day, holy to the Lord; and that the right celebration of this day consisteth in a spiritual communion with God, our own souls, and each with other in all gospel-ordinances, and other Christian offices, of goodness and mercy to man and beast, as opportunity and Christian prudence shall require."[62]

In addition to the charge of degrading the Sabbath, Bellamy alleged that the Particular Baptists condemned the practice of psalm-singing.[63] Quoting from Ephesians 5:19, Cheare and Steed affirmed the practice of psalm-singing. The purpose of singing the psalms, they went on to reason, was for the worship to God and for the edification of the church. The content of singing was limited to "the songs of Moses, David: or otherwise, as the Spirit bringeth things to their remembrance, and gives them utterance."[64] Only an "amen" or "hallelujah" was permitted at the conclusion of the song. Musical instruments and solo voices were not allowed, because they were part of the first administration of the covenant. Yet, it was

---

60. Ibid., *Plain Discovery*, 15.
61. Bellamy, *Leper Cleansed*, 5.
62. Cheare and Steed, *Plain Discovery*, 5.
63. Bellamy, *Leper Cleansed*, 12, 16; Cheare and Steed, *Plain Discovery*, 41.
64. Cheare and Steed, *Plain Discovery*, 42.

entirely appropriate and essential to use "the common artificial rhymes, measures, and tunes."[65]

Another allegation hurled at the Particular Baptists was that they verbally abused those who were strict in observing the spiritual disciplines.[66] Cheare and Steed affirmed, "We faithfully exhort unto these Christian duties, we reprove their neglect; and are in a readiness to pass public censures upon the careless and willful transgressours of them, as persons offending against plain precepts."[67] At the same time, they cautioned that a "Pharisaical strictness in polishing the outward-man by the traditions and inventions of men . . . and a formal strictness in the letter of a command" are "desperate enemies to the Gospel of Christ."[68] What Cheare and Steed were driving at *in nuce* was the avoidance of two extremes, legalism on the one hand and antinomianism on the other.

They proceeded to stress the importance of the church in the formation of biblical piety in its members. Piety was not merely an individual effort, but it was to be nurtured in conjunction with edification and communion within the context of a local church.

> That our selves might be built up, and be helpful each to build up other in the faithful exercise thereof without distraction, hath been one main motive to draw us into the union and communion in which by the grace of God we stand, and is a part of that promise, which we through the Lord's assistance (the God in covenant with us) do declare and undertake when we receive the right-hand of visible fellowship together.[69]

To another of Bellamy's specific charges, that Particular Baptist families neglected "family-duty" and were "without prayer generally, their children without instruction; and surely their constant neglect of duties in their families", Cheare and Steed responded: "The Lord knoweth we long and labour to have our houses as churches of Christ, and our children in submission with all gravity, brought up in the nurture and admonition of the Lord."[70] And in response to Bellamy's indictment that the Particular Baptists made prayer a matter of liberty rather than duty in the family, they

---

65. Ibid., *Plain Discovery*, 42.
66. Bellamy, *Leper Cleansed*, 5.
67. Cheare and Steed, *Plain Discovery*, 6.
68. Ibid.
69. Ibid.
70. Bellamy, *Leper Cleansed*, 5; Cheare and Steed, *Plain Discovery*, 6.

maintained that "it is the duty of parents and masters fearing God, to be frequent in calling their families together, instructing them in the principles of religion; endeavouring by all means possible, their conversion and salvation, and in their presence to spread their condition before the Lord; praying for them, that God would set home such instructions and endeavours with power."[71] They explained further that families were obligated to observe specific spiritual disciplines. While this was the general desire of all Particular Baptists, Cheare and Steed humbly acknowledged that it was not realistic for church leaders to stringently regulate spiritual disciplines in their parishioners' families. They promised, however, to Bellamy that "a more strict enquiry after all neglects of that kind" would be made so that the pastors could "help them and us unto a more thorough reformation."[72]

Lest one conclude that Cheare, Steed, and the Particular Baptists considered themselves the epitome of spirituality and *sine culpa*, they realized that they were rife with imperfections and weaknesses. "[We] know our selves to be a weak and dark people," they admitted, "yet we declare, that through the supporting mercy of God, whom we fear, and on whom in this day of rebuke and blasphemy, we rely for help, we shall not cease to witness before great and small, as the Lord shall minister ability, and clear up our way."[73] Their statements demonstrated a commitment to exercise church discipline for even neglect of spiritual duties. This commitment stemmed from the Particular Baptists' belief that God "placeth some special men over the Church" for the purpose of "the keeping of this church in holy and orderly communion."[74] These "special men," pastors, were to "govern, oversee, visit, watch; so likewise for the better keeping thereof in all places, by the members, he hath given authority, and laid duty upon all, to watch over one another."[75] Cheare and Steed took the formation of spiritual piety within the church seriously and believed that it was the duty of both the ministers and the members to make improvements in their piety. By these responses to Bellamy's accusations of both doctrinal infidelity and spiritual apathy, Cheare and Steed aimed to defend and demonstrate "the true state of our doctrine, way, and practice, as it stands accused and judged by him."[76]

---

71. Cheare and Steed, *Plain Discovery*, 43.
72. Ibid., 6–7.
73. Ibid., 77.
74. *First London Confession of Faith* 44 in Lumpkin, *Baptist Confessions of Faith*, 168.
75. Ibid.
76. Cheare and Steed, *Plain Discovery*, 1.

Conclusion

Laboring as a minister in Plymouth, building networks of partnership among Particular Baptists, promoting ecclesiastical unity, and preserving doctrinal purity, Cheare succinctly summed up his life in three words: Christian, minister, and sufferer.[77] As a minister, Cheare did not limit his labor and influence to his own Plymouth congregation. He avoided the pitfall of insularity and sectarianism, seeing himself as a minister of the broader church, the church universal. He encouraged other Particular Baptist ministers to follow his example. In light of the doctrinal differences and debates of his day, he accepted with gravity his responsibility to "cry aloud, and spare not; [to] lift up our voice like a trumpet . . . to set up the house of our God and to repair the desolations thereof."[78] Cheare's unflagging commitment to build the Particular Baptist churches of England into "a compact and knit city" serves as a model for us today. As Cheare admonished the churches to abolish their independent mindset, so should churches of all generations resist the temptation to be insular and rather to embrace the concerns of the broader church while being faithful to the gospel.

---

77. Cheare, *Words in Season*, 182.
78. Cheare, *Sighs for Sion*, 14.

3

"Waiting on the Spirit of Promise": Abraham Cheare in Prison in the 1660s

THE POSTHUMOUSLY PUBLISHED PRISON writings of Cheare were compiled in *Words in Season* and *A Looking-Glass for Children*. Comprised of three sections, *Words in Season* began with Cheare's personal, almost biographical, treatment of Hebrews 11:35, setting "forth the incomparable excellency of faith" in the midst of tortures.[1] The second section, "The Embalming of a Dead Cause," was an exhortation from Cheare addressed to fellow Christians suffering persecution by the government to allow themselves "to be vindicated by the Lord, to whom their integrity is known, and their cause committed."[2] The final section of the work was a compilation of various letters and sayings, including Cheare's last words on his deathbed. Notable in this section were his exhortations to parents to raise their children so "that your houses may become as so many churches of Christ in respect of that instruction, reading the Scriptures, praying, gracious conference, discipline, exemplary walking in all holy conversation and godliness."[3] Though Cheare apparently had no children of his own, these parental letters along with his *A Looking-Glass for Children* revealed Cheare's warm affection for children.

The latter compendium, a collection of poems and hymns designed for children to learn and memorize, demonstrated Cheare's proclivity to express great truths in verse. In fact, so masterful and influential was he in this genre that it drew the attention of Benjamin Keach, who, in the

---

1. Cheare, *Words in Season*, 1.
2. Ibid., 110.
3. Ibid., 224–26.

introduction of his 1691 edition of *Instructions for Children*, stated, "Moreover I would have you get that little book called, 'A Token for Children' and another called, 'A Looking-Glass for Children.' Next to your Bible, pray read them pretty books."[4] Composed specifically for youth, "calling them early to remember their Creator," Cheare's works for children were the first known hymns composed for children and they adumbrated John Bunyan's *Country Rhymes for Children*.[5] The content of this collection was vast in its scope, ranging from topics on piety, conversion, and the Bible to evil company and eternal damnation. Included in this compilation were some personal poems expressing Cheare's suffering as well as those written as eulogies for some of his deceased friends.

The Nature of Persecution

In the first two sections of *Words in Season*, Cheare unpacked his theology of persecution along with sharing his personal experience of the nature and psychology of persecution. Addressed to his congregation, which had been harassed by local authorities in Plymouth, his writings on the subject were infused with a thoroughly sensitive, pastoral tone. Cheare honed in on two timeless concerns regarding the persecution of God's people, namely, the nature of their persecution and the dilemma of deliverance from persecution.

In addressing the nature of persecution, Cheare delineated the sources and causes of persecution. First, he attributed persecution to human depravity, "the beastly nature and lust of poor fallen man, that bears the image of the devil herein."[6] Wicked men were "brutes," "wild beasts," "lions," and "wolves," despising God and those who follow Him.[7] Their revulsion for the truth was particularly exacerbated "by the holy conversation of testifying saints," as the purity of the saints exposed their baseness.[8] Therefore, evil men expressed their ire by wreaking havoc on the saints. Cheare also traced the genesis of persecution all the way back to the Garden of Eden. When God placed enmity between the seed of the woman and the seed of the serpent, a "perpetual discord" between God's people and His enemies

---

4. Cited in Foster, "Early Baptist Writers of Verse," 102.
5. Martin, "The Baptist Contribution to Early English Hymnody," 195–96.
6. Cheare, *Words in Season*, 12.
7. Ibid.
8. Ibid.

was born.[9] Persecution of the saints, thus, stemmed from the "old hatred" displayed by the devil in the Garden and will not cease until "the God of Peace tread[s] Satan under our feet, which will be shortly, till that old serpent, which is the devil and Satan, be bound and cast into the bottomless pit."[10] Third, persecution sometimes arose from those who zealously, even sincerely, served God. However, their blind zeal, like the Apostle Paul's before his conversion, caused them to commit heinous acts against the saints. As Cheare put it: "They who think it promotes divine service to persecute saints, being zealous of a traditional worship of their fathers, will be very cruel in their undertakings . . . This, when it comes to be the guise of persecutors, will make of it fierce times."[11]

As his fourth cause, Cheare discerned that the boldness of God's people often triggered their persecutors' "wrath boiling up to torment."[12] Cheare cited the biblical examples of Mordecai and Stephen, men who remained steadfast, possessing a "constant, bold, and courageous spirit" in spite of the enemy's fury. Embedded in this discussion was a pastoral word to Cheare's parishioners who were facing threats and arrests by the local magistrates. Cheare exhorted them to persevere in their boldness for the sake of the gospel. Instead of catering to the desires of their persecutors by accepting their terms of deliverance, they were "rather to wait on the Lord with the more earnestness to double and multiply his Spirit, and the strengths and consolations of it with us."[13] Finally, Cheare viewed the absolute authority of government, when wielded by evil men, as being a cause of brutal, widespread persecution of the saints. At this juncture, Cheare became very personal, as he hinted at the abuses dealt to him and other Nonconformists by the English Parliament. Government leaders, he averred, had "a providential admittance to the capacity of making laws, and putting them in execution against the people of God, having their own lusts uncontrollable, and an advantage of covering their cruelty under pretext of law, and to asperse the faithfulness of saints to the laws of Jesus Christ."[14] What made their display of authority so revolting for Cheare was their execution of it in the name of God's authority that was delegated to them. Thus, they indicted God's

9. Ibid., 13.
10. Ibid.
11. Ibid., 14.
12. Ibid.
13. Ibid., 15.
14. Ibid.

people with "the odious charges of being against magistracy, and not being subject to the higher powers, the old accusation."[15]

With the causes of persecution established, Cheare then listed possible purposes that God had for His saints in allowing persecution to occur. Again with deeply pastoral overtones, Cheare began by stating God's designs in the negative. Persecution was not a result of God's delight in witnessing His own suffer affliction for His sake. Neither should it be attributed to God's lack of affection for them. He explained:

> It goes (as we may speak with reverence) near the heart of the Lord to see his jewels thus dealt withal . . . Nay, he hath testified the greatest displeasure against such as have been executioners of his rebukes, when they have not performed them with pity. His anointed ones must be very tenderly handled, and have no harm done against them, wheresoever they wander.[16]

God's purposes in permitting persecution, therefore, were all positive, reasoned Cheare, for he "hath higher and better ends to promote than their deliverance; ends that have more of good in them that these tortures can possibly have of evil."[17]

As his first stated purpose, Cheare argued that in allowing persecution God intended to accentuate the inestimable value of biblical truth. Persecution enabled all people, both the persecutors and the persecuted, to witness the infallibility of God's truth through the lives of his saints, an occurrence that would otherwise be inscrutable. Second, Cheare drew attention to God's designs in establishing grace in the hearts of his persecuted saints by using persecution as his instrument to that end. While Satan attempted through persecution to obliterate all grace within the saints, God strengthened the work of grace that was already operating within their hearts. Third, God used persecution to display his power in preserving his saints from breaking down and casting away their own faith. What greater occasion, reasoned Cheare, than in times of persecution when his saints "have no external props to stay them up" does God have to evince His power?

---

15. Ibid. Cheare, in support of "the old accusation" of "being against magistracy," included Nehemiah 2:19, 6:6, and Acts 17:6–7. These biblical references are examples of God's people being accused for inciting rebellion and sedition as well as rejecting political authority.

16. Cheare, *Words in Season*, 20–21.

17. Ibid., 21.

> As long as times and providences hold to keep off pains from the body, chains from the legs, stripes from the back, famine from the belly, other props and principles may be presumed to bear one up: but when there is no fruit in the vine, no flock in the field, no herd in the stall, none shut up nor left, yet then to rejoice in the Lord, to glory in tribulation, to accompt it all joy to fall into divers of them, and they great ones; this is convincing, that such are kept, and kept up by the mighty power of God.[18]

In addition to the aforementioned purposes, Cheare suggested that God had a specific purpose ordained for the persecutors. Through the vehicle of persecution, God exposed the wickedness of humankind in general, attesting to all that he is the Righteous One and the legitimate Ruler of all. The extreme cruelty utilized in persecuting the saints can even be used to praise God and to cause all men to "breathe after the Lord's arising to rule the earth, and become the Governor among the nations."[19]

"Faith's Conquest"

From delineating the nature of persecution with its sources and divine purposes, Cheare then shifted to a topic of great pastoral import for the persecuted saints of his era. It was not sufficient alone for saints to know the causes and purposes of their being the objects of persecution. Something tangible and relevant was essential to enable them to live through times of trial. Cheare contended that the possession of faith was indispensable for the endurance of persecution. From Hebrews 11:33–35, Cheare observed that it was imperative that the "tortured, butchered, massacred, harmless, weak" saints embrace the "noble and glorious principle," faith, which was "of invincible power to make them conquerors in all their tortures."[20] His discussion of the faith of believers in persecution was comprised of two salient points. First, the possession of faith was essential in that it established the truths of Scripture within the souls of the afflicted saints. Second, faith bestowed encouragement and perseverance through the most intense and bitterest of persecutions.

Cheare noted three specific areas in which faith clarified certain biblical truths and secured assurance in the soul. Faith reminded the saint of

18. Ibid. 24.
19. Ibid., 25.
20. Ibid., 2–3, 39.

the truth that a union existed between his soul and Jesus Christ. This was of the utmost importance in the midst of persecution when the temptation to doubt God's steadfast love was more present. When, by faith, the believer lived in assurance of his relationship with Christ, "the soul becomes impregnable."[21] Another truth that faith confirmed in the soul, submitted Cheare, was the legitimacy of the gospel cause for which the saint was persecuted. It was a common temptation for the persecuted saint to question the validity and value of the gospel in the midst of suffering. But faith assured the believer that the cause of Christ was indeed a *bona fide* and noble cause. Third, faith bolstered the saint's assurance that his persecutors were in the hands of a sovereign God and were, ultimately, at his disposal. When he viewed his persecutors through the eyes of faith, he saw "abundance of wind and emptiness in all the threatenings of the sons of men."[22] The terms of deliverance that they offered and dangled before the saint was, in reality, a "vapour."[23] Furthermore, their offers and promises of liberation from persecution were poisonous delicacies, for "a bow or cringe at a distance may seem a small matter, for the obtaining such advantage, but Christ sees it too great to give to Satan, for the gaining the glory of earth or heaven either."[24] These things the persecuted saint observed through faith and thereby gained assurance and comfort that his suffering had spiritual benefit.

In addition to establishing the truths of Scripture within the believer's soul during persecution, faith provided encouragement through even the direst of persecutions. Cheare submitted four words of pastoral import regarding the impact of faith upon a soul during persecution. First, through supernatural means, faith produced an inexplicable composure within the saint who underwent the torture and agony of persecution. Faith in God's goodness yielded a sweet peace as the saint's thoughts turned from himself to God. In only a way that can be described in spiritual terms, "when thus the mind [of the persecuted saint] is quiet, the man is invincible."[25] Faith, furthermore, graced the saint with a spirit of submission to God. Cheare described this "resignedness" to God, reflecting his own experience:

21. Ibid., 40.
22. Ibid., 43.
23. Ibid., 44.
24. Ibid., 45.
25. Ibid., 46.

> [Faith] brings the soul up to a certain resignedness unto God, to a willingness to be at God's dispose; here am I, let him do with me what seemeth good in his sight: That which makes torments to be tortures indeed, is when the members draw one way, and the mind another; but when the soul comes to be fully yielded up to divine pleasure, this makes tortures become no tortures, or at least to become less tortures.[26]

Cheare pointed his readers to Christ, who modeled a calm disposition and submission to his Father in declaring, "For this cause came I to this hour, Father glorify thy Name" (John 12:27–28),[27] Just as Christ did not resist his Father's plan to suffer at the hands of evil men, so saints were to experience sweet submission to God while suffering persecution.

In his third point, Cheare observed that the possession of faith produced a boldness of spirit to endure the most vicious of persecutions. Instead of shrinking back or recanting, the saint with faith acted with boldness until either God intervened or brought him to himself. Cheare, again revealed his boldness for Christ as he exhorted his readers to embrace the same faith that produced this kind of mettle: "I have now an opportunity, which I may never have again, to play the man, the Christian, the believer, for my God, my Christ, for his Gospel, his institutions, his cause and interest. What can be too hot or heavy to be done or suffered upon this accompt?"[28] Faith also sustained the persecuted believer by enabling him to get a glimpse of the glory that is to come. Cheare set before his readers Christ, Moses, Stephen, and the saints of the Ancient Church as those worthy of emulation in this regards, because they caught "a fore-taste of that better resurrection, realizing and rendering substantial the promised glory thereof unto it.[29]

The Dilemma of Deliverance

A substantial portion of *Words in Seasons* was devoted to the highly controversial subject of deliverance from persecution. As previously noted, Cheare had wrestled over this issue of deliverance during his imprisonment as he was offered at least on one occasion to take the Oath of Allegiance,

26. Ibid. 47.
27. Ibid.
28. Ibid., 49.
29. Ibid. Cheare cited from Hebrews 12:2, 11:26–27, 10:34, and Acts 7:55–56.

which would have secured his freedom. In the first section of *Words in Season*, Cheare gave no intimations or possibilities of accepting any offers of deliverance from persecution until half way through his argument. However, Cheare introduced the possibility of accepting the terms of deliverance within clear and explicit parameters. Posing this possibility late in his argument seems to be indicative of the fact that he believed that his personal context did not qualify for accepting any offer of deliverance. Yet he did entertain the possibility and explained that under certain circumstances it would not only be permissible, but even obligatory to accept such an offer.

Cheare asked his readers to consider an offer of deliverance in theological terms. If the terms of deliverance were legitimate and did not compromise the gospel, then "that deliverance (as deliverance may be considered) is a mercy not to be refused, but accepted by believers."[30] Cheare explained further: "So is it a very high duty incumbent on such to receive deliverance at the hand of God; then to accept deliverance is his duty, and to give it such acceptance and entertainment in truth."[31] The believer was to view the deliverance "as something conveyed to him by the goodness of a good God."[32] Furthermore, every believer will give an account to God not only for acts committed, but also for acts received or rejected, including offers of deliverance. It was essential, therefore, that the saint consider any valid offer seriously and accept it. "As he must reckon for every idle word, and all the deeds done in the body," Cheare wrote, "so he must yield an account of all his receipts whatever they be, and therefore must so receive and improve as one that must be judged by the law of liberty."[33] But what if the believer refused to accept divine deliverance? Cheare had three strong words for those who would embrace persecution with high-handed arrogance. First, that believer was "a mere destroyer of himself; a thing abhorrent to godliness."[34] Refusal of such deliverance, Cheare observed, was tantamount to abusing the temple of God, which 1 Corinthians 6:19 taught was the body. Abusing or destroying God's temple, therefore, was a grave sin that would be judged. "If life, liberty, or any mercy may be had in God's way," Cheare insisted, "the refusal of it is the destroying [of] our selves so far as that mercy extends.[35] Second, refusal to accept legitimate deliverance

30. Ibid., 58.
31. Ibid., 60.
32. Ibid., 58.
33. Ibid., 60.
34. Ibid., 61.
35. Ibid.

"Waiting on the Spirit of Promise": Abraham Cheare in Prison in the 1660s

from persecution revealed a heart of ingratitude to God, who providentially provided a respite from the persecution. For the believer "to scorn or set at nought his [God's] favours, is very much beneath the ingenuity of a believer."[36] Third, Cheare solemnly warned the believer that if he refused deliverance, he would be accountable for his neglect of and irresponsibility to his family and any other dependents he had. As Cheare explained, "So if he draw them into sufferings, from whence he might have deliverance in a way honorable and acceptable to the Lord, he is accessory of their misery, their wrong will be upon him."[37]

Following these three words of warning, Cheare proceeded to address a pastorally complex issue, one concerning the inner motives of the persecuted saint. Before he delineated the motives proper, he began with a refutation of the notion that godliness could be equated with persecution.

> Godliness, and the profession of it, doth not inevitably run and necessitate a Christian upon the hazard and loss of every thing he hath, or induce him to cast away all . . . Do not therefore take up hard thoughts of godliness, because of the doctrine of self-denial, the cross at entrance, or the trials and tribulations that are appointed to attend the professors of it.[38]

Cheare was not discounting the fact that godliness may require the "casting away" of all through persecution, but he was affirming that it did not necessarily follow that godliness exclusively demanded suffering. Godliness could frequently entail pleasures and enjoyable things in this life, averred Cheare. What Cheare was driving at was exactly what the Apostle Paul articulated in Colossians 2:18–23. Asceticism from all creature comforts did not lead to or equate with godliness. All things, whether persecutions or pleasures, were to be received with gratitude and accompanied by a spirit of submission. This was true godliness.

With these prefatory remarks stated, Cheare then demonstrated that suffering persecution did not automatically elevate a believer to godliness, for there was the possibility of him harboring ulterior motives that bore the mark of ungodliness. Cheare cautioned his readers that there existed multifarious, implicit reasons why some believers persisted in their suffering from persecution rather than accepting deliverance. One common motive, he pointed, was the desire for self-righteousness, which ever lurked in the

36. Ibid.
37. Ibid., 62.
38. Ibid., 62–63.

heart and manifested itself in the deceptively subtle attempt "to establish a man's own righteousness in opposition to the righteousness of Christ in the Gospel: its wonderful to consider what tortures it will wade through in compassing its design…Men have, and do admit great hardships on their body, to promote the righteousness of the flesh."[39] And this lethal self-righteousness could display itself, even in persecution! Another reason that some saints persevered in persecution was the desire to be affiliated with a particular cause more than with Christ. Cheare cited the disciples in John 11 who volunteered to die with Lazarus and who also later claimed they were willing to become martyrs with Jesus (Luke 22:33). Cheare's point was that some believers possessed an unholy lust for persecution, because they thought it would gain them an advantage with certain people or ministries. Last, some believers who reached a point of desperation in their suffering would even choose to remain in their persecuted state hoping to die, because they had given up the desire to live. This suicidal motive hardly commended itself as a noble reason to stand fast in times of persecution.

While Cheare recognized that God did intervene and provide opportunities for deliverance from persecution, the bulk of his discussion centered on the refusal of offers of conditional deliverance, for the acceptance of such would besmirch the name of Christ. Speaking to his context of the Act of Uniformity and the subsequent Great Ejection, he submitted a more comprehensive critique of deliverance including a thorough treatment on the theology of deliverance from persecution.

He commenced his critique with a general proposition that served as his application from Hebrews 11:35, "some were tortured, refusing to accept release." Cheare argued from this reference that it was incumbent on his Christian readers to refuse deliverance under the given political circumstances in England with the exception of unconditional terms of deliverance as previously noted. The saint, Cheare explained, ultimately had one of two offers before him to accept: the offer of conditional deliverance from physical torture on the terms of acquiescing to the government or the offer of the Comforter, who promised not only physical deliverance, but the prospect of the resurrection. Though the latter offer, acknowledged Cheare, may bring about an increase of pain, it was the "glorious resurrection that will repair all tortured bodies, tottered limbs, [and] massacred members."[40] Cheare advised his readers, in spite of the many voices that pled with them

---

39. Ibid., 64.
40. Ibid., 56.

to save themselves, to solemnly consider and weigh these two options, but ultimately, to trust God with their lives.

> Look to your choice, let your choice be the off-spring of a well-deliberated and digested judgment upon the case… Scorn the torturer, slight the tender; reject the offer at man's hand, it is and hath a lie in the right hand: fall into the hands of the Lord, commit the keeping of thy soul to him in well-doing, as into the hands of a faithful Creator: be assured he is able to keep that which is committed to him against that day. This is an hard saying, flesh cannot bear it, but faith can and doth.[41]

With the context of rejecting deliverance introduced, Cheare raised a single question that was doubtless posed to him by persecuted saints. His meticulous answer was marked by pastoral insight and counsel for those who suffered not only physically, but mentally and emotionally from persecution. The question was: what were the factors that compelled one to persevere in persecution rather than to escape it by accepting deliverance? Cheare's answer, outlined in several stages, was accompanied by possible objections from persecuted believers, who wrestled with the tempting prospect of being liberated from their torture. First, deliverance was to be rejected if the acceptance of the terms involved the committing of some sin, for "there is more of evil in the least sin, than there can possibly be of good in the greatest deliverance."[42] A potential objection to Cheare's counsel was that it was legitimate to choose the lesser of two evils, hence, to accept freedom from persecution was justified. With an introduction to this ethical dilemma, Cheare countered this objection by repudiating any consideration to choose evil: "For a man is not to commit the least sin, to avoid the greatest suffering; no nor to commit one sin to avoid another… God doth not need any sin of ours to promote any end of his, nor any proper end of ours."[43]

Second, Cheare urged his readers to abandon any deliverance that would cause them to sear their conscience, which "is the best friend thou hast under heaven."[44] An anticipated cavil to his point was that other godly saints had acquiesced and their consciences, which permitted them to do so, remained unscathed. To this, Cheare responded that if the truth were

41. Ibid.
42. Ibid., 73.
43. Ibid., 74.
44. Ibid., 78.

told, those saints, more than likely, had the appearance of a clear conscience, but "one may discern them to have pale faces, which may give intimation, all is not well within."[45] Cheare explained the tragedy of the irreparable damage to one's conscience by accepting an illegitimate offer of deliverance. "Take heed therefore by the force of others," he counseled regarding the conscience, "or the fear and treachery that is in thy self, thou admit any violence done to it, lest once stretching it beyond its staple, it never do the offices of a good conscience more to thee, to counsel, excuse, witness toward thy peace more."[46] Another clear indicator of whether one should accept or refuse deliverance was the possibility of causing others to be scandalized and potentially fall into sin. Cheare had these severe words for the saint who would accept deliverance for himself, yet not give due consideration to the souls of others affected by his acceptance:

> I confess there is a great latitude of liberty wherein a Christian may walk in lawful things, among which the obtaining deliverance is a branch of privilege: but if it be attempted, as by many 'tis, to the offending, wounding, destroying of many of Christ's little ones; a millstone hung about the neck is more tolerable than the consequence of such attainments.[47]

Thus, Cheare concluded that deliverance in the main should be eschewed at all costs, for it was "a crust for a dog (saith Luther of the Turkish Empire) a feast too empty to satisfy an immortal soul."[48]

Cheare as a Model of Piety amidst Persecution

Both *Words in Season* and *A Looking-Glass for Children* are replete with numinous depth and piety. In these writings, Cheare particularly provided an exemplary model of piety in the context of suffering and persecution. Cheare distinguished piety from religion, for "there was much talk of religion in the world, but few had attained to acquaintance with the powerful inward part of it."[49] Cheare's piety manifested itself in three specific ways. First, Cheare demonstrated a marked humility, even when enduring in-

---

45. Ibid.
46. Ibid.
47. Ibid., 88.
48. Ibid., 102.
49. Ibid., 190.

tense torture and suffering for his convictions. Cheare acknowledged his own weaknesses as he wrote, "I need your prayers and precious exhortations, tending to prevent slumber, that I be not taken at unawares."[50] His view of his role as the minister of the Plymouth church was telling when he shared his deep sense of being inadequate for ministry. He viewed himself as "so unsuitable to a door-keeper there ... such a worm ... I prove but an heap of infamy."[51] On his deathbed, he requested to his friends, "When I am gone, speak moderately of me I beseech you; but if anything hath been seen in me worth learning, let it be offered with much humility; or rather I think, let my works praise me in the gate."[52]

Second, throughout his suffering, Cheare possessed a remarkable perseverance. Aiding this perseverance was his view that suffering was a means of deepening piety. As debilitating as the sufferings were with regard to his body and as wretched as his environs were, Cheare looked beyond his external circumstances and regarded his desolate abode as a sacrosanct haven where his sufferings were actually nurturing the Spirit's heart-work within him: "Soul-searching, heart-preparing, sin-mortifying work, may have more advantage from the retirement of a nasty prison, than (unless abundance of grace be ministered) from being left to walk in a large place."[53] Of course, there were times when the nastiness of his surroundings deeply depressed him. On one occasion, he noted that the spiritual "filthiness" of many of his fellow prisoners and guards "with their oaths, curses, singing, roaring, raging" would make his circumstances "a prison indeed" were it not for "the goodness of God, and of his cause" that enabled him to stand fast.[54]

On his deathbed, he reflected upon the spiritual benefit he had received from his suffering, "God hath reserved this proof of my ministry until these few years last past, having been little acquainted with sickness before."[55] Clouds, he attested, were necessary in promoting a vital spirituality:

> I had no cloud on my peace, and joy in the Lord, since this sickness; but have seen cause since to change my voice in that matter, the Lord having since that, brought me under trials and cloudings

50. Ibid., 245.
51. Ibid., 240.
52. Ibid., 189.
53. Ibid., 252. See below, p. 95.
54. Ibid., 272.
55. Ibid., 190.

sometimes, though blessed be God, they have been day, not night-clouds, through which God hath shined; and I cannot so much desire for myself or others, that we might always be without clouds, as that our holiness might be promoted, and carried on by them, then all will be well.[56]

Cheare found invigorating hope in the Bible as a result of his sufferings and it, in turn, impacted his piety.

> When floods and multitudes
> Of troubled thoughts me press;
> I call to mind, thy word, and find,
> Its joys my soul refresh.
>
> And though in scorn and pain,
> Forsook, and poor I be,
> Thy word alone, hath all in one,
> Health, wealth, friends, all to me.[57]

Furthermore, Cheare not only believed his suffering enriched his own spirituality, but he also concluded that others reaped blessings from his trials. Writing to a close pastoral friend in 1664 while in the Exeter jail, he explained: "Your sufferings may be the conversion of others . . . thy suffering for Christ may be the best sermon that ever thou preachedst in thy life, and may win more upon souls; as we say, The best living, is the best preaching; so I say, To suffer well is the best preaching."[58]

Third, submission to God in his sufferings was central in Cheare's life. Suffering, though painful, was not to be shunned; rather, it was to be embraced. As Cheare reflected on his suffering, he expressed in riveting language his contentment in the will of God for his life.

> Very well satisfied, all have been steps of divine ordering; I would not have come from Exon [i.e. Exeter], might I have had my own will; I would not have stayed in Plymouth, a'ter I had preached once, but God would have me stay; I would not have come to this place, after my time of suffering was out in the Town-Hall at Plymouth, if I might have had my own will; but God would bring me hither, and bless be the Lord that let me not have my own will,

---

56. Ibid., 198.
57. Cheare, *Looking-Glass*, 36–37. See below, p. 76.
58. Cheare, *Words in Season*, 256–57.

> blessed be God that brought me here, and blessed me here . . . the steps of God have been in great wisdom with me, and the bottom of them all paved with love.[59]

Even when death was imminent, he confessed he was still learning that "God hath been many ways bringing me to an acquiescence in his will . . . by bringing this poor body under such straightening circumstances."[60] Arresting in its power and imagery was a verse that Cheare penned on 17 September 1665, ten days before he was sentenced to exile on Drake's Island:

> And thought not then, I here again,
> A month's restraint should find,
> Since to my den, cast out from men,
> I'm during life design'd.
> But since my lines the Lord assigns
> In such a lot to be,
> I kiss the rod, confess my God
> Deals faithfully with me.
> My charged crime, in His due time,
> He fully will decide;
> And until then, forgiving men,
> In peace with him I bide.[61]

Conclusion

Approximately four days before his death in 1668 as he lay ill, worsening in his prison cell on Drake's Island, Cheare mustered enough strength to utter before his friends a jeremiad against the nation of England, which had persecuted and expelled so many of her godly ministers including Cheare himself.

> Oh! poor England, sinful England, who stonest the prophets, and choice men that are sent unto thee, but wouldest not hear in this thy day, the things that appertain unto thy peace; but now they are hid from thine eyes. Thou hast had an iron sinew and brow of brass, and wouldst not be gathered to the great Shepherd and

---

59. Ibid., 183–84. See below, p. 87.
60. Ibid., 201.
61. Cheare, *Looking-Glass*, 86. See below, p. 80.

> Bishop of Souls. Ah England! England! What would many kings, and princes, and righteous men have given to have enjoyed, one of those blessed days of the Son of God, which thou hast sinned away, and rendered thy self unworthy of? Oh! how art thou become a place of persecution, treading and trampling down God, his name, and concerns, as much as in thee lies![62]

Then addressing his friends present in his cell, he charged them to have a courageous spirit and to be faithful to God in spite of the persecution that threatened them. He beseeched them to "make religion your business, and that you make not godliness a slight thing, nor walking with God a small matter, as ever you hope to stand with boldness before God in the judgment."[63] At this poignant moment, Cheare then requested that his friends raise his hands up in Aaronic fashion as it were and be his witnesses as he delivered his final charge. The editor of *Words in Season*, perhaps present in the cell, observed that Cheare, with elevated hands, pled with them to "make it their great business, the remaining part of their days to walk, to the praise and glory of the Lord Jesus, in all the paths of his pleasure."[64]

Cheare, to the very end, "kissed the rod" of suffering, not with rash temerity or arrogance, but rather with a firm conviction that his suffering was for the cause of the gospel. To surrender to the desires of his persecutors was to "betray the Lord's interest . . . step aside from the Lord's precepts, and make invalid the Lord's promises."[65] Though his refusal to accept deliverance on the terms of compliance to the Act of Uniformity ultimately broke his health and drove him to an early death, Cheare looked beyond his earthly suffering in a "nasty prison" and saw the hope of a better resurrection, which was, he said, "a doctrine of unspeakable strength and encouragement to the Lord's suffering, banished, tortured ones, as many in this day have found it."[66] It was with this faith in the resurrection of the body, accompanied with his boldness for the gospel, that he whispered his final words in response to a friend, who recited to him Psalm 34:5, "They looked unto the Lord and were lightened." Cheare replied, "Yea, and their faces were not ashamed."[67]

62. Cheare, *Words in Season*, 205–6.
63. Ibid., 206–7.
64. Ibid., 207.
65. Ibid., 91.
66. Ibid. 104.
67. Ibid., 217.

4

A Letter of Abraham Cheare on Baptism, c. 1648–1658

One of the ways in which seventeenth- and eighteenth-century Baptists sometimes defended believer's baptism was to relate accounts where a sick individual was baptized and then subsequently healed. Andrew Gifford, Jr. (1700-1784) who pastored a Baptist congregation in London—his grandfather, also called Andrew Gifford (1649-1721), would have been well known to Cheare since the elder Gifford was the pastor of the Pithay congregation in Bristol—preserved the following letter by Cheare about a baptism and healing of a certain Captain Francis Langdon in Cornwall.[1]

A BRIEF NARRATIVE OF some occurrences, relating to that memorable transaction of the Lord's providence, in owning of his despised ways and people, in a miraculous preservation and wonderful restoration of the sick body of our brother, Captain Langdon, upon his obedience unto the Lord, in submitting unto that ordinance of baptism, although, as to the outward appearance, all hope of his surviving it was lost. You may peradventure have heard, how greatly the Lord was pleased to satisfy the spirit of our dear brother, Captain Langdon, about baptism, at our brother Steed's (of Bovey), late (lately) being there, only that, having a consumption strong upon him, he waited for a word of faith to give strength to his weak body to follow

---

1. From Nicholson, *Authentic Records*, 13–17. Francis Langdon represented Cornwall in the Barebones Parliament of 1653–1654.

See also the letter of Andrew Gifford, Jr. describing a similar healing after baptism in Ivimey, "A Wonderful Appearance," 257. The Victorian Baptist author G. Holden Pike regarded this link between baptism and healing as a "delusion" and verging on fanaticism ("A Western Pastor in the Olden Time," 407).

the Lord. Since which time, although his consumption grew strong upon him, yet withal the Lord was pleased to engage his heart under a necessity of following after him therein, and not only so, but there grew up with it a very strong persuasion that upon baptism he should be healed of his distemper, of which he became so exceedingly confident, that he admitted of no thought to the contrary, but declared it to all people that came to visit him, which were many of all kinds, that seeing the clergy and their adherents had so shamefully vilified that ordinance, the Lord would now signally appear to own it, and that, not only to make them appear to be liars that say it was a murdering act, but would also show that Jesus of Nazareth had healing virtue to convey thereby to him, when all his strength was gone; for he told them he should be weak even to the point of death, and then upon baptism the Lord would show his strong arm. The reporting of this his confidence, as it was a great grief to divers about him, fearing it was some mistake as theirs was, Acts 22:4; and thinking what dishonour it would bring upon the truth if the Lord should not appear as he expected—so was the enemy heightened exceedingly and filled with mocking at it, which also caused many strong cries to go up night and day that either the Lord would abate of our brother's confidence, if it were not of him, or else provide with stretched out arm for his name.

Whereupon he sends for me, three weeks before this meeting, to this end, and I did set on as far as here[2] but was strangely turned back by a whole series of strange providence, and could not break through again till the very time of the meeting, when I was brought thither and met Colonel Bennatt[3] and divers friends, his wife and daughter, brother Muckle and brother Frenchick, and divers friends from all quarters. The state I found the man in, was thus, a sentence of death, in his and every beholder's eye, passed upon him. All doctors left him, his breath had almost left him, his speech hardly to be perceived, scarce able when he was in his chair to rise upon his feet, and if up, hardly able to step one step without being held up, the very sinews of his neck loosed, that his head hung in his bosom, cough tearing him even to pieces. He had not slept one hour in many nights, only two or three times the week before, as a return of prayers in the particular case put up for him by the servants of the house, at his desire; he could receive in no nourishment but a little milk, he had utterly laid aside all cordials. And indeed when I saw him at first, I thought he would hardly live

---

2. Cheare must have been absent from Plymouth when this request reached him.
3. This is Colonel Robert Bennet. See above, p. 12.

till the morning, this was his outward estate. As for his spirit it was fully set, and that without wavering, upon the Lord, it is a most clear evidence of Divine sealings, his resolutions fixed to be baptized, and his confidence that suddenly upon baptism he should be healed. This he propounded to me, together with the grounds of persuasions and laid it upon me as such a duty as I ought not to scruple to perform, though he had not been out of his chamber for many weeks. Before, he could not endure the least air, yet now a sharp eastern wind, a notable frost in January.

The place [was] about a half mile from his house, being Millpool in the highway. The spectators and expectors, some hundreds of people, the mutterings of some that if he died upon the action the life of the minister should be questioned, he also tells me he would presently send for brother Steed or brother Forty, to come over to him and do it. What my straits were and the straits of all such as had the name and glory of God in their eye, you may in part imagine. As the case is now freely hinted, especially theirs, who have in some cases heretofore, observed his exceeding confidence to be rebuked with miscarriages and disappointments. Yet unless you had been present and a close observer of these and many other occurrences, that made the case on both hands difficult, you cannot possibly conceive how great my perplexities were herein. Well, a great part, if not all the first night after I came, was spent in prayer jointly and privately about the thing, my soul exceedingly clouded and unable to see through it, but having divers others considerations such Scriptures as these seemingly set on me, the Lord requires mercy and not sacrifice, expecting what a man hath and not what a man hath not, but principally, thou shalt not tempt the Lord thy God. Of this persuasion also were many of the most staid saints, Colonel Bennatt, Major Bowden, brother Stevens, brother Frenchick, brother Chapman, and divers others, on the other hand, sister Kockwish, Mary Bowden's sister Prudence, Cook and some others, very spiritual souls that had prayed much about it, had persuasions together with him he should be healed; a third party brother Frenchick and brother Muckle and several others, had faith enough to the performance of the duty, though not for the healing, they being persuaded that he would not be worse for baptism, but that God would vindicate his ordinance in the sight of all beholders, that it was not of itself destructive to any faithful, obedient person. Many hours were spent in prayer and the matter cast upon the Lord, with as much necessity to plead for his glory and answer his people, as I met with in any case since. I believe the man grew all this while apparently weaker, decayed more in one day now, than in a week before. Sleep seemed to have taken his farewell, and his voice itself, that he spake as one in the greatest of hoarseness, strength left him more and more, yet will he not hear of a denial, nor of a delay, nor of any expedient as to get water in the house to do it, but in the manner and way aforesaid.

Sister Prudence's daughter-in-law and another of the family propounded for baptism, he tells me he shall be ready as soon as they, that as soon as they come out of the water he will come in unto me and require me to do my duty, and in case I would come out and leave him there so it should be. We go down into the water, I baptized these women, he is brought to the water side on his horse, his man riding behind him, keeping him in his arms, and requires me to do my duty, I told him I had not faith, he then requires brother Muckle, standing by, that if he had faith to do his duty he should perform it, brother Muckle goeth down with him into the water, and he is led by two or three men, he baptizeth him. Immediately as soon as he is out of the water, he requireth that no person hold him, but strongly, swiftly as one that runneth, he goeth up alone against the hill which was very steep, 50 or 60 feet, and then was led and helped home, declaring that he found at that instant—recovery. He is put into his bed, speaketh strongly and heartily, after the Lord was waited upon for an hour, he calleth for victuals, desires beef and pork, afterwards lieth him down to sleep, and sleeps very well all that night for the space of seven or eight hours; had not one straining pull of the cough that night, when he waketh, he saith, he could have slept longer, but was unwilling to have the friends depart till he had spoken of the salvation of God. He is very hearty all the morning, ariseth about noon, but tarried not long up, saying, he found the bed more comfortable than the fire, and I think had some faintness, but still declared that he lived by faith to have the cure perfected by degrees, as his weakness grew by degrees. He rejoiced much that the Lord had so manifestly owned his ordinance, he seemed to be humbled for his confidence that he should be perfectly sound, presently desires the saints for to exercise faith and prayers for his complete healing.

Thus I left him and came away, what effects the sight of this whole affair wrought is not yet. I am persuaded in the full intent of it manifested marvellous astonishment upon us all. Five present themselves, in the morning I came away, and I saw them baptized by brother Muckle, viz— Mary Bowden's eldest son, and an ancient woman near 80 years old, deaf, leaning upon a staff; a very choice experience named S. Simons, one Mrs.

Harris, and a servant man and maid of the house, most of them wrought upon by this man's labour, a most choice gospel worked upon them all, as I have heard, many more were in readiness, only Satan keeps them off with slender excuses. Colonel Bennatt's daughter offered herself to be baptized but, for some reasons that had weight in it, its deferred till next time I come where she is. Young Mr. Trisies under great convictions about it. Major Bowden saith he is very nigh it; there is a great people made ready for the Lord. I received the last night a letter from brother Muckle, whom I left with his wife in the place—he writes, "My brother Langdon is more recovered in his body since I was there, they hope he grows better and better; he is better now since his baptism than he had been many weeks before." He was baptized the 7th of this instant. Hitherto God hath helped us.

SIGHS for SION,
OR,
FAITH and LOVE

Containing some grievings in her Sorrow, and groanings for her Deliverance:

By a few of her weak and unworthy Children.

Humbly, and in all faithfulness, presented to those Assemblies of hers, where Grace hath set them as Watchmen; and unto any others, that in every place call upon the Name of JESUS CHRIST our Lord, both theirs and ours.

In way of ESSAY,

To blow the Trumpet in Sion, and sound an Alarm in Gods holy Mountain, To the awakening them that are at ease, and pressing and encouraging all the upright in heart, to be in pain with her, in this day of her sore travel, and great Expectation.

PSAL. 137. 1. —— *We wept, when we remembred Sion.*

ISA. 62. 6, 7. *I have set Watchmen upon thy walls, O Jerusalem, which shall never hold their peace day nor night: ye that make mention of the Lord, keep not silence, and give him no rest, till he establish, till he make Jerusalem a praise in the earth.*

LAM. 2. 18, 19. *Their heart cryed unto the Lord: O wall of the daughter of Sion, let tears run down like a river night and day, give thy self no rest, let not the apple of thine eyes cease; arise, cry out in the night, in the beginning of the watches pour out thy heart like water before the face of the Lord, &c.*

MIC. 4. 10. *Be in pain and labour to bring forth, O daughter of Sion, like a woman in travel.*

ISA. 96. 8 —— *As soon as Sion traveled, she brought forth her Children.*

LONDON,
Printed for *Livewel Chapman* at the Crown in Popes head alley. 1657.

5

Abraham Cheare, *Sighs for Sion*[1]

To the several congregations respectively, to which we stand especially related; viz. In Plymouth, Abingdon, Totness, Bovhey-Tracy, and Dartmouth.

Dearly Beloved,
We know, and acknowledge our selves to be debtors (yea, we owe our own selves) to the Lord, and you, for the exceeding grace that we (though most unworthy) have found in his sight, counting us faithful, and putting us into the ministry of his Gospel; and for that our service amongst you hath been, and is in any measure accepted. Under the sense of which engagement, it is the least we can do, to be ready to render an accompt of our selves from time to time unto you; the which we the more cheerfully now undertake, as being under the persuasion of a call of the Lord, leading us forth thereunto, and having good hopes, through grace, that our labour shall not be vain in him; in and through whom we are,

Yours, faithfully labouring (though in much weakness) for your souls' prosperity, as those whose joy and rejoicing, both here, and in the day of Christ, wait to be fulfilled therein.

Abraham Cheare, Henry Forty, John Pendarves, Tho[mas] Glasse, Robert Steede.

---

1. Cheare, *Sighs for Sion*. The entirety of this tract is reproduced here.

The great God of heaven and earth, who hath graven you, O ye precious sons and daughters of Sion, on the palms of his hands, hath also greatly endeared you to our hearts; insomuch as we may say with the Apostle, Ye are in our hearts (in the Lord) to live and die with you;[2] yea, we trust our inward affection is more abundantly toward you, than our visible expression in the ensuing lines: whereof at present we find no better testimony wherewith to present you, than that which is here tendered to your view: Your candid acceptance of so poor a mite, with a favourable construction, and a due improvement of this word in season, to the glory of God our Father, and the comfort of you his dear children, will be that wherein our desires and ends will be answered, and our souls encouraged in the work of God, and your work; with resolution in the power of God to hold on therein, passing by evil and good report, yea, and gladly to spend and be spent for Christ's sake, and for your sakes, who are Christ's.

But here we must begin with judging our selves, and covering our faces with deserved shame, that we who have stood forth so long to minister the Word among the saints, and to make mention of the work of God: and have yet had so little searchings of heart in the matter that is now before us; have known and felt so little, not only of the power, but even of the form of this blessed work, so as either to stir up and engage our own hearts, or to provoke the churches of the saints unto their concernments of this nature: But have rather eased and pleased our selves and others, in discoursing of, and prosecuting some other things, though good in themselves, and in their places, yet such as wherein our private interest of peace and comfort is more sensibly wrapped up; in the mean time falling short of (at least not so self-denyingly reaching after) the advancement of that name, interest, and glory of God, that should be upon our hearts, to have made manifest in all the earth, from the rising of the sun, and from the west.[3]

And as we cannot but be sensible of the narrowness of our own spirits, with grief, and shame; so also, as that which is weighty on us, we do observe, That a self-seeking and self-pleasing spirit, hath taken great hold of, and advantage on many professors these days; witness their little naturally-caring for Sion's state, most seeking their own things, and so few seeking the things of Jesus Christ, and of their brethren, for edification. And Oh!

---

2. 2 Cor 7:3. The biblical references that are cited are, for the most part, found in the margin of *Sighs for Sion*. A few, where it is clear that a quotation is being made, have been added.

3. Isa 59:19.

that there were not among you, even among you, who are the churches of Christ, cause of complaint in this respect.[4] These things we mention, not to cast reproach upon you, but with grieved hearts, God knoweth. And now, that we might discharge, and have the answer of a good conscience, in following the Lord fully, we have taken the opportunity of this work, that we trust himself hath been fixing on our spirits, after seeking to God, and waiting upon his majesty, To beseech and provoke you, and every one of you, as you have any fellowship with Christ our Head, by faith, or in and with his body, the church of the first-born, by love, you would for his, and his Sion's sake, hear, and receive our exhortations, considering with weighty spirits what we say: and the Lord give you understanding in all things.

The cause then that we desire with trembling to plead, (brethren) is Sion's, even hers, whom men have called an out-cast, saying, This is Sion, whom no man seeketh after;[5] and of whom that ancient lamentation may in a great measure be taken up, as verified in this our day, There is none to guide her among all the sons whom she hath brought forth, neither is there any that taketh her by the hand, of all the sons that she hath brought up; among all her lovers she hath none to comfort her, &c.[6] And her professed friends, (many of them) have dealt treacherously with her, and are become her enemies.

Dear souls! our request on her behalf is, that you would look upon Sion, that city of our solemnities, of whom glorious things are spoken, and laid up in promise for her, even to the rendering her the perfection of beauty, An eternal excellency, The joy of many generations.[7] And oh! that your hearts may be so suitably affected with an holy sympathy in her state, through that one Spirit that is in promise for all her children, that you may truly say, as souls whom faith and love have transported into her interest, All my springs are in thee.[8]

But lest we be mistaken in your thoughts, while we speak of her in that figurative term; and to the end our apprehensions may be distinct and clear, in our wrestlings together on her behalf, we pray you to consider what we intend and mind in the expression [Sion.]

---

4. 2 Chron 28:10.
5. Jer 30:17; Isa 51:18.
6. Lam 1:2.
7. Isa 33:20; Pss 87:3, 50:2, 48:2; Isa 60:15.
8. Ps 87:7.

First, Sion considered in a more large sense, takes in the whole election of God, Whose names are written in heaven, that whole body for which Christ gave himself, and whereof Christ is given to be Head; not only those who have believed, but those also who shall believe, for whom, as Christ hath prayed, That they all may be one, as the Father is in him, and he in the Father, that they may be one in them, that the world may believe that the Father hath sent him: so ought we to strive mightily with God, and them, travailing in birth for them, till Christ be formed in them all; enduring also all things for their sakes, that they also may obtain the salvation which is in Christ Jesus with eternal glory.[9]

But secondly, by Sion, we here intend more especially and particularly, God's called and faithful people, Jews and Gentiles, fellow-citizens in Christ, even the whole Israel of God, as considered or concerned in a controversy with Babylon, stated in the Scriptures; taking in, as well those of that blessed family, who are now in heaven, for the avenging of whose blood, we ought without fainting to cry day and night, as the peculiar people of God upon the face of the whole earth; even all that in every place call upon the name of the Lord out of a pure heart:[10] in whom the glory of God is more highly concerned, than in all things else in the world, not only in his pleading thoroughly their cause in all the controversies of Sion with her adversaries, but also in beautifying her with his glorious presence, and restoring her to her primitive glory, in respect of a pure gospel-faith, union, and order; wherein being found as a blessed bride, prepared for the coming of the glorious bridegroom, she may be counted worthy of all that glory that shall be brought unto her, at the second appearing of Jesus Christ, now drawing nigh.

This blessed people, this Sion, God's glorious building, and workmanship in Christ, the true seed of Abraham, and heirs of the promise, both Jews and Gentiles; however in the issue they shall be a name, and praise to him in all the earth: And although this great work in and for them, be still before him; yet is it the wisdom and good pleasure of the Father, in the depths of his everlasting counsel, to let the manifestation of it in the world, and his dispensations about it, be very various, and seemingly to carnal eyes, unsuitable to such intendments, through the many deaths, distresses,

---

9. Heb 12:22–23; John 10:16; 2 Tim 2:19; John 17:20–21; Col 1:29; Gal 4:19; 2 Tim 2:10.

10. Eph 2:19, 3:15; Gal 6:16; Isa 34:8; Luke 18:7–8; Rev 18:20, 24; Ps 73:1; Rom 10:12; Jer 50:34.

and unlikelihoods, with which he cloatheth it in their sight: the which he turneth nevertheless to the exceeding advantage of his name all along, not only by exercising thoroughly the patience, obedience, and faithfulness of his children, in owning the truth of his testimony, and bearing their testimony for him unto the death; but withal, by giving full occasion, and opportunity, for that mystery of God to be finished, who hath testified, and declared by the Spirit of prophecy to the churches, and permitteth by an hand of Providence, the rising, and raging of that man of sin, that bloody mystery of iniquity, until it have answered and fulfilled whatsoever is held forth of it, in all the various Scripture-prophesies, figures, and representations both of its civil and ecclesiastical concernment.[11] The which, as it hath gotten to its height both of renown and cruelty, by the occasion of that exceeding great offence, wherewith the cause of Christ hath been presented in its appearance to the world, being a stumbling-stone to the children of this worlds wisdom and glory: So shall its ruin arise from that jealousy of the Lord wherein he hath promised to plead the cause of his own, and his people's glory; finding in, and recompensing on that generation, on whom the hour of his wrath shall fall, all that righteous blood that hath been shed, and all that unworthy and treacherous usage that Sion hath met withal in the days of her poverty and distress.

The day of Sion's full deliverance, the destruction of her enemies, and the setting up of Christ's glorious kingdom, is very much upon his heart (Isaiah 63:4) as a fruit of the sore travail of his soul (Isaiah 53:11,12) and recompense of that unworthy usage that himself, his cause and people have had upon the earth; and for which, sitting at the right-hand of God, he is in continual expectation (Hebrews 10:13) as that which must be given him as a fruit of his intercession (Psalm 2:8,9) and to which he is preparing his way, by terrible things in righteousness (Psalm 65:5,8) shaking both heaven and earth, and making a quick dispatch (Luke 18:7,8) ordering, and ruling all things therein, and making them subject to this his great and glorious work.[12] And indeed, so much the more is this design and work declared to be upon his heart, as the whole management of it will lie upon his own shoulders; they being very few among men, that will be found to have regard to it, in the budding of it; not only through the blindness and enmity of those that are aliens from him, but the very great sleep and slumber that will be found among them that pretend to him, either through their want of faith

---

11. Isa 49:14–16; Mic 4:11–12; Rev 13:10, 14:12.
12. Isa 49:7, 61:3, 7.

(Luke 18:8) or their sensual engagements in this present evil world (Luke 17:26).¹³ So that notwithstanding that salvation he works for them, and his pleading their cause, lays them under no small engagement to him, when his cause comes to be pleaded, the complaint is made by the prophet (Isaiah 59:16), And he saw that there was no man, and wondered that there was no intercessor. Therefore his arm brought salvation unto him. The which great defection even of saints themselves, from following the Lamb in this special service, together with the fixation of the work upon the heart of Christ notwithstanding this, serveth highly now more than ever, the day drawing nearer, to commend, and greatly to encourage and excite the faithfulness of any, though the weakest and most despised of the Lord's holy ones, who are in a right spirit engag'd for, and together with Christ, in their constant waitings, and fervent expectations of this manifestation of his glory: they hereby witnessing that they have the mind of Christ; and having one mind, give their power and strength to the Lamb, as called, and chosen, and faithful, (when others have one mind to give theirs to the beast) making prayers also for him continually, and preferring him and his interest before their chief joy, through the spirit of faith and love; always reckoning themselves as being in the body, and members in particular.¹⁴

A taste of this worthy Spirit (brethren, beloved in the Lord) we humbly trust our God is giving us, who address our selves to you, with some fervent desires that we may be made more to partake of it. And indeed, such is our love to your souls, and delight (through grace) in this work before us, that we cannot but commend it to you, with more than an ordinary importunity; beseeching you, and every one of you, from the greatest to the least, notwithstanding divers differences amongst you, touching the time, way and manner of God's effecting those great things, that by the will, and in the way of the Lord, you be found reaching after the same Spirit, and wrestling much together and apart for it. And Oh! that it may be the pleasure of the Lord herein, that your zeal may provoke many, and you may be found to have stood in this hour of temptation, and this backsliding time, faithful with the Lamb on the Mount Sion, having not only His Father's name written on your foreheads, but his work graven upon your hearts, and all those blessed characters disposing you thereunto, shining in all your conversations; which will make you covet, that the Lord make his work appear to you as his servants though he reserve the revelation of his

---

13. Isa 9:7; Ps 132:17.
14. 2 Cor 2:16; Rev 17:14, 14; Ps 72:15, 137:6, Heb 13:3; 1 Cor 12:27.

glory unto your children.[15] For what greater joy, or crown of rejoicing, can we have at the appearing of our Lord, than that we with you, and ye with us, be presented faultless before his throne? whereunto we also labour, and desire to strive mightily, according to his working.[16] In which work, and to which end, we pray you bear with us, while we follow this exhortation a little further in a few words.

Is not the exercise of such a public spirit for the whole work of the Lord most desirable? if we consider farther, not only its sweet likeness unto, and fellowship with the heart of Christ; but withal, that very great blessing that hath been promised, and all ages they have found to their particular souls, who have been given up to mind most naturally, and follow most fully, that design of God, that had its present tendency in that very age to promote Sion: the Lord is not unrighteous to forget such work, and labour of love, that is shewed towards his name.[17] How hath that word been made good to them that pray for her peace, They shall prosper that love thee?[18] And see, we pray you (dear brethren) how God hath bid his choice remnant to consider, and reckon from that very day, wherein they set their hearts and hands about the work of Sion, from this day will I bless you (Haggai 2:18,19) what choice testimonies of the great love of God to himself, did Daniel find at several times! He is said to be a man greatly beloved, or a man of desires (Daniel 9:23, 10:11,19) when he was wrestling for the name and work of God singly, not minding a word of his own interest (that we read of) farther than it was wrapped up in the Lord's? besides the great secrets that were opened to him, of the deep designs of God for a great while to come. What a desirable foresight had David given him by the Spirit, in all the pattern of the house of the Lord, and large furnishings thereunto? yea, what provision, to his astonishment, did God make for building him an house, and establishing his kingdom, when in the time of his rest he was taking care of that house of God's glory, because of which all the people of the earth might know his name?[19]

What a constant observation was Nehemiah enabled to take of the hand of God for good upon him (Nehemiah 2:8,18) and what boldness, and

---

15. 2 Cor 9:2; Rev 14:1; Pss 84:5–7, 90:16.
16. Jude 24; Col 1:28.
17. Isa 66:10; Zeph 3:18; Heb 6:10.
18. Ps 122:6.
19. 1 Chron 6:33.

clearness of access, and appeal to the Lord, was he still furnished withal, while he was in the fear of God (Nehemiah 5:9,15) about the work of Sion?[20]

Was not Ezra's experience much of the eye and hand of the Lord accompanying him, in all that great work he did for the Lord his God?[21]

Moreover, it deserves our serious observation, being written for generations to come, how much the Lord is delighted in the faithful fervent prayers of those who have sought him, in behalf of the people called by his name; in that he hath carefully preserved the memorial of them, causing them to be expressly recorded in his book; as appears in the first of Nehemiah, and the ninth of Daniel: all which, with many others that might be named, are ensamples unto us, that we by their pattern might be stirred up to serve our generation, with faithful spirits, by the will of God.[22]

To which also we might add, the remembrance of the curse on them that hate Sion; yea, the apparent withering and blasting that hath been, and is on them, that in following their private interests, neglect her, and defer her work, under this pretence, The time is not yet come, the time that the Lord's house should be built; whilst in the mean time they prefer their relations, possessions, and other worldly accommodations, before this dear interest of Jesus Christ: for which, that judgment in a spiritual sense is come upon some, and may justly be feared as coming on others (Haggai 1:10,11).[23] The heavens over them are stayed from dew, etc. Yea, and hath not God punished this neglect in many, with such a decrease of their spiritual moisture, as that word is made good in them (Psalm 137:6). Their tongues even cleave to the roofs of their mouths; whilst others, faithful in improving their received measure of a spirit of faith and prayer, are abundantly increased therein. Oh! what dreadful woes are pronounced to them that find their pleasures in such a season, but regard not the work of the Lord, nor consider the operation of his hands; that are at ease in Sion, but are not grieved for the afflictions of Joseph; careless daughters, that lay not to heart the perishing of the righteous, and consider not the taking away of the merciful men; with whom the Lord will plead, as with them that sport themselves against him: the desire of such slothful ones will kill them (Proverbs 21:25) and their prosperity destroy them (Proverbs 1:32).[24]

20. Neh 5:19, 6:9, 13:14, 22, 31.
21. Ezra 5:5, 7:6, 9:8, 8:18, 22, 31.
22. Ps 102:17–18; Acts 13:36.
23. Ps 129:5; Hag 1:2–11.
24. Isa 5:11–12, 23:12–14; Amos 6:1–6; Isa 32:9, 11; 57:1, 4.

And now, brethren, is it not high time, that we cry aloud, and spare not; lift up our voice like a trumpet, when it is too too evident, that in the day of a little ease wherein for a little space grace hath been given us from the Lord our God, even a little reviving in our bondage, to set up the house of our God, and to repair the desolations thereof, men are sleeping, lying down, loving to slumber in every corner, saying, It is not nigh; let us build houses? etc.[25] And is not pride, and fullness of bread companions to this abundant idleness, through which the building decayeth?[26] Oh that at length, for the Lord's sake, we might be provoked to be fervent in Spirit, serving the Lord, and that knowing the time, that now it is high time to awake out of sleep: for now ours, and Sion's salvation, is nearer than when we believed.[27]

For the quickening of our hearts to this work, and the heightening of our expectations therein, hath not the Lord given us, among many other, this remarkable sign of the times, even a mighty spirit of faith and prayer, through some choice discoveries of grace raised up in his people? by the exercise of which, in the management of Sion's controversy, great and glorious wonders have been wrought in these nations, by unlikely means, in answer to the prayers of the saints; as hath been openly confessed by the instruments employed, which have caused themselves, and others, beholders, to stand amazed thereat: and although many who once seemed to be pillars in this cause, have soon forgot these great works, and have turned back from following fully after God in this way; yet there is a remnant, a generation that remain upon their watch tower, with whom the hand of the Lord rests wonderfully, upholding their faith and hope for Sion, notwithstanding all discouragements, in their incessant prayers for her. Hath God said to his at any time, Seek ye me in vain? (Isaiah 45:19) hath not God by evident answers of prayers in these days, sealed it in a good measure to his people, that the time to favour her, yea the set-time is come? for he hath regarded the prayer of the poor destitute, and hath not despised their prayer: and is not this written for our sakes? (see Psalm 102:17,18) God who beautifieth his mercies to his people, by giving them in their due season, having in these latter days given forth this glorious blessing of a spirit of grace and supplication so abundantly, and continuing the same, hath he not some great work to be further carried on thereby?

25. Isa 58:1; Joel 2:1, 15; Ezra 9:8–9.
26. Ezek 16:49; Prov 18:9.
27. Rom 12:11, 13:11.

Oh! that we could present unto you, in a lively way, what our souls have begun to taste of those first ripe fruits, of that arising and growing Spirit, that grace hath in a measure visited some saints withal, that have jointly and severally desired to be found faithful for the Lord: they have to our abundant refreshing witnessed that their labour is not in vain in the Lord; nay, in keeping such commandments there is great reward: whilst they have felt (though as yet it be but a little of) Sion's pangs upon their hearts, they have been strongly carried up into the spirit of that day, and their souls were made as the chariots of Amindadab: which declareth clearly to us, that were we but put into perfect travail in our spirits, did we take pleasure indeed in her stones, and favour the dust thereof, it would turn to us for a further testimony, that the time of God's arising to shew mercy to Sion, the time to favour her, yea the set time were come.[28]

But alas for us! we have not only sought our ease when pain should have been upon us, but as foolish children, have stayed long in the place of the breaking forth of children; and by the iniquities that we have contracted since we were named Sion's children, we have kept back good things from her: what remaineth now, but that we lay her state so much the more deeply to heart, as we have drawn grief upon her, and added to her deformity?[29] being earnest in a spirit of faith and prayer night and day in her behalf, as becometh children nursed at her side, suitably affected, and acted with and for her: not expecting our own deliverance, any other way than in hers, knowing that we without her cannot be made perfect.[30]

And that we hold on our way without fainting, & not be in our mournings as men without hope; would it not prove of great advantage, to the raising and keeping up our faith, to be much exercised and delighted in the prospect that is to be had, through the promises, into her (ready to be revealed) glory?[31] However, her visage is now blacker than a coal; she is not known in the streets: treacherous dealers have dealt very treacherously with her; a disappointment hath befallen many of her hopeful expectations, because her transgressions are many: reproach hath befallen her at the hands of professors; and the enemies that know not the Lord, blaspheme.[32] The light and Spirit of the Lord is belied and abused by vain men, unsound in

---

28. Song 6:12; Isa 66:8; Ps 102:13–14.
29. Hos 13:13; Jer 5:25.
30. Esth 4:13–14; Heb 11:40.
31. Luke 18:1.
32. Lam 4:8; Isa 24:16; 59:9, 11.

the faith, disobedient to, and despisers of the precious ordinances of Jesus Christ; through which also, loss of children hath here and there betided her assemblies. Yet hath Jehovah spoken it, and his faithfulness is engaged in an everlasting covenant, that though she hath been forsaken and hated, that no man went through her, yet he will make her an eternal excellency, a joy of many generations, the city of the Lord; the Sion of the Holy one of Israel shall she be called; in nothing more glorious, than in the perpetual presence of her King, and God with her, who shall tabernacle with men, and dwell with them, they being his people, and he himself shall be with them, and be their God, being in stead of a temple, sun, and moon; the glory of God and Lamb always lightning her, the Lord being her everlasting light, and her God her glory.[33] How amiable in the day of her deliverance, shall Sion be, through the bringing to her glory that ancient people, the family of Abraham, God's friend, when they shall see him whom they have pierced, and mourn for him, and be saved by him in that great day of Jezreel, the Lord uniting Ephraim and Judah, making them very great, holy, and a blessing round about? (Ezekiel 34:26).[34] And what shall the receiving of them be, but life from the dead? (Romans 11:15) and when the glory of the Lord shall be risen upon her, then shall the Gentiles come unto her light, and kings to the brightness of her rising (Isaiah 60:1,3). Yea, from the rising of the sun, unto the going down of the same, shall the name of the Lord be great among the Gentiles; all nations flowing unto the mountain of the Lord, when it shall be advanced to the tops of the mountains, and exalted above the hills: yea what glorious things are said of this city of God?[35] There shall be births in Rahab, and Babylon, Philistia, Ethiopia, and Tyre; and yet when God shall count up the people, he shall say of Sion, This and that man was born in her, and the highest himself shall establish her (Psalm 87:3–5) the zeal of the Lord of hosts shall do this. And Oh! that all the Lord's people were so fully prepared, as a bride, to meet their blessed bridegroom; that we might all unfeignedly say with one accord, Even so, come Lord Jesus, come quickly.[36]

Had we but truly noble spirits, how would these discoveries of glory ravish us, and our eye affect our heart? setting us with restless spirits, to be looking for, and hastening unto, that day of the Lord; this day of the

---

33. Isa 60:14–15; Zech 2:10; Ezek 37:27–29; Rev 21:3, 21–23; Isa 60:19–20.
34. Zech 12:10; Hos 1:11; Isa 11:13; Jer 3:18.
35. Mal 1:11; Isa 2:2.
36. Rev 22:20.

manifest exalting Jesus, as King of saints, and King of nations?[37] Nay, would it not fill our hearts with jealousy for his name, against all that standeth up in the earth, to oppose his kingdom glory, beginning at home in our own spirits?[38] the zeal of the Lord's house would eat us up, and the love of it would crucify us more unto, and wean us from those interests of earth, and men, whereupon we have been apt to lean, and whereunto we have been deeply and dangerously engaged: causing us also to wait to be with Jesus, which is best of all; and in the mean time to pant, and thirst incessantly, for that holy Spirit of promise, that alone can present us with the ravishing glory of that expected day, and raise up our spirits to a sweet and suitable disposition, according to the will of God, to wait and act aright toward it.[39]

Dear hearts, let your faith be high, and your wrestlings without weariness; neither be ye in any measure discouraged, nor discouraging one another: in this matter the strong cannot say to the weak, I have no need of thee; should not all our interest in heaven be improved to the uttermost, in this day of Jacob's trouble?[40] Oh strengthen the weak hands, and confirm the feeble knees (Isaiah 35:3). Provoke one another to this love, and these good works; say to one another, Let us go speedily to pray before the Lord, and to seek the Lord of hosts; I will go also.[41] And ye, O poor of the flock, that wait upon the Lord, and know that this is the word of the Lord, be strong, yea, be strong and of good courage; knowing, that in this work of God's tabernacle, he receiveth in good part your sincere, though weak, breathings; your badgers-skins, and goats-hair, is in no wise cast out.[42] Ye that are of a fearful heart, be strong, fear not: behold, your God will come with vengeance, even God with a recompense; he will come and save you (Isaiah 35:4). What shall one then answer the messengers of the nations? That the Lord hath founded Sion, and the poor of his people shall betake themselves to it (Isaiah 14:32).

And ye also, beloved and honoured brethren, who minister the Word of grace among the saints, How comely will your goings be, as he-goats before the flocks, in this work? Have you not the prophets of old, who have spoken in the name of the Lord, for an example; whose words accompanied

---

37. 2 Pet 3:12; Isa 33:18.
38. Rev 15:3–4.
39. Ps 69:9.
40. Num 6:32; 1 Cor 12:27.
41. Heb 10:14; Zech 8:21.
42. Zech 11:11; Exod 35:21, 23.

with the same Spirit of faith, will they not furnish to this work? In reading their writings, consider their work in such a time as this, (professors then being in such a posture of security as now) was it not to warn them (with a woe unto them) who were at ease in Sion (Amos 6:1, 3–4, etc.) and such as regarded not the work of the Lord, nor the operation of his hands? (Isaiah 5:12) Which duty had they neglected, would not God have required it at their hands? Did they not call upon the people to assemble together, to fast and pray, to mourn and weep before the Lord, to plead the cause of his people, his heritage? (Joel 2:15–17) Thus did they, whose example is laid before you, as wise stewards, giving to those of the household a portion, suitable to the present season. Should we not resemble them in this, crying out with the watchmen upon Mount Ephraim (Jeremiah 31:6), Arise ye, and let us go up to Sion, unto the Lord our God; withal, waiting daily on God for such a discerning of the times, as might render us like the children of Issachar, who knew what Israel ought to do? (1 Chronicles 12:32) If this rude essay, or small tinkling (as it may be judged) may provoke you, who are more skillful, to blow the trumpet, and the Lord spirit you thereunto, do it, we pray you, as for his, and his people's sake, with all your might; not sparing to lay out your more worthy labours, for the carrying on of this work. Bear with us, yet a little, in our humble importunity: Is not the glorious name of God, the peace of Jerusalem, and its prosperity, the prosperity of your own souls also, and the people to whom you relate, who may be discouraged by your remissness, eminently concerned in this matter? Yet once more, we beseech you therefore, in the bowels of Christ, let not any worldly interest, prejudice, jealousy, fear of ill events, or any carnal reasoning whatsoever, withhold your hearts or hands, from helping in so good and glorious a work.

What shall we say more, dearly beloved? if there be any consolation in Christ, if any comfort of love, if any fellowship of the Spirit, if any bowels and mercies, fulfill ye our joy, in being of one accord, and one mind, in this weighty work commended unto you; wherein the name and glory of God (which ought to be dearer to us than our lives) is so eminently concerned.[43] And withal, add to your diligence, in looking into the concernments of Christ, and his saints, that having arrived unto a distinct knowledge of them, your hearts being duly affected with them, you may go on prosperously, not only to spread before the Lord, both his, and his people's cause, as the matter shall require; but also wait for the return of prayer; discerning

---

43. Phil 2:1–2.

this in your selves, That they best know how good God is to them that seek him, that after seeking, wait for him (Lamentations 3:25,26).[44] Having been thus bold with you for Sion, we humbly crave for our selves, That we may be had in especial remembrance on your hearts before the Lord, that we may be fitted for, and faithful in the work of our dear Redeemer: Into whose embraces we give you up, and remain,

Your poor unworthy brethren, through rich grace firmly knit unto you, in the bonds of Gospel-love; and one with you in your spiritual warfare, and waiting for the exaltation of Jesus Christ,

Abraham Cheare, Henry Forty, John Pendarves, Tho[mas] Glasse, Robert Steede.

---

44. 1 Kgs 8:59.

6

Abraham Cheare, *A Looking-Glass*

Remember now thy Creator in the days of thy youth.[1]

1.
Sweet children, Wisdom you invites,
to hearken to her voice;
She offers to you rare delights,
Most worthy of your choice.
Eternal blessings in his ways,
You shall be sure to find;
Oh! therefore in your youthful days,
Your great Creator mind.

2.
The joy that other pleasure brings,
with vanities abound:
Nay; when in straits they take them wings,
vexations they are found.
Your very vitals thus decays,
and torments leave behind:
Oh! therefore in your youthful days,
your great Creator mind.

---

1. Cheare and Jessey, *Looking-Glass*, 21–24.

3.
They may affect depraved sense
while they subject your reason;
They say, to conscience, get you hence,
and fear it for a season.
But though a kind of sottish ease,
you hereby seem to find,
I beg you in your youthful days,
Your great Creator mind.

4.
The dreadful danger heed I pray,
of such strange ways at length;
When you have sin'd your time away,
and wasted all your strength;
Be sure, in chains of darkness, these
your hands and feet will bind:
Oh! therefore in your youthful days,
your great Creator mind.

5.
Observe how poor mortal men,
their precious seasons spend,
To satisfy those lusts, but then
must perish in the end.
This saving counsel, would you please
upon your heart to bind:
Oh! in your early youthful days,
your great Creator mind.

6.
Upon a world, vain toilsome, soul,
a journey now you enter:
The welfare of your living soul,
you dangerously adventure
If as the issue of your ways,
you've happiness design'd:
Oh! in your early youthful days
your great Creator mind.

7.
Friends, parents, all who you affect,
observe your budding spring;
Your prosperous summer they expect,
a fruitful crop will bring:
A witness in this age to raise,
to grace of every kind:
Oh! then in these your youthful days,
your great Creator mind.

8.
Young Isaacs, who lift up their eyes,
and meditate in fields;
Young Jacobs, who the blessing prize,
this age but seldom yields.
Few Samuels, leaving their plays,
to temple work resign'd:
Few do, as these, in youthful days,
their great Creator mind.

9.
Now precious Obadiahs be,
that feared God in youth;
How seldom Timothys we see,
versed in the Word of Truth.
Few babes and sucklings publish praise,
th'avengers rage to bind.
Oh! then in these your youthful days,
your great Creator mind.

10.
Few tender-hearted youths, as was
Josiah, Judah's King;
Hosannah in the high'st (alas)
how seldom children sing?
Youths rarely ask for Zion's ways,
they'd rather pleasure find:
But oh! in these your youthful days,
your great Creator mind.

11.
What children pulse and water choose,
continually to eat;
Rather than conscience should accuse,
for tasting royal meat?
Would you not bow, a king to please,
though tortures were behind?
Oh! then in these your youthful days,
your great Creator mind.

12.
Those worthy mirrors of their age,
obtain'd a precious name;
Their living pattern should engage
your souls to do the same.
And though in this strait narrow way,
you few companions find;
The rather in your youthful day,
your great Creator mind.

13.
How worthy Christ is, could you learn,
to claim your flower and prime;
And how well pleasing 'tis, discern
to dedicate your time:
You pleasantly would make essays,
to get your souls enclin'd,
And gladly in your youthful days,
your great Creator mind.

14.
This garland wreath'd of youthful flowers
to Jesus you would bring:
This morn made up of golden hours,
you would present the King.
You'd humbly bow, without delays,
Grace in his sight to find;
And gladly now, and all your days,
your great Creator mind.

A Letter sent to a friend's child.[2]

(Introduction)
Sweet child. I pray you, think not long,
E're I have sent my prison song;
To turn, after a godly sort,
Your tongue, and thoughts, from sinful sport.
Pray let it frequently be brought,
With holy fear upon your thought;
And when indeed your soul is bent,
On things that are most permanent.
When least to foolish mirth inclin'd,
Then from the treasure of your mind,
This serious song, you forth may bring,
With Gospel melody, and sing,

Lord what a worm am I?
what could'st thou here espy?
That ever thou, should'st humbly bow,
On me to cast an eye?
What kind love is this?
What reason can it have?
Shall God through grace, himself abase,
So vile a wretch to save?

How strangely was I made?
How curiously adorn'd?
I was at first, an heap of dust,
Which sin hath quite deform'd.

My matter, earth and clay,
Form'd by a power divine:
Sure God would hide, all cause of pride
From every thought of mine.

2. Ibid., 29–31.

Waiting on the Spirit of Promise

My childish thoughts would cease,
On vanity to stay,
Could I bethink, I'm on the brink
Of danger day by day,

Temptations lead to sin;
Sin doth of good bereave me:
Clothes, beauty, strength, and life at length
Are all at hand to leave me.

Why then should gay attire,
Yield so much food to pride?
What glory's in a beauteous skin,
That so much filth doth hide?

Why should the fond delights
Of parents puff me up?
Such boundless love, doth often prove,
To both a bitter cup.

Why should the highest joys
Of sin subject my reason?
The sinful sports of princes' courts,
Last only for a season.

Lord let my soul be rais'd,
And all its power incline.
On eagle's wings, to follow things,
That are indeed divine.

Those depths that from the wise
Thou pleasest to conceal;
Mysterious things, obscur'd from kings,
To me a babe reveal,

That from an infant's mouth,
A suckling's lips inspir'd;
Thy glorious name, may purchase fame,
And Christ be more admir'd.

Let me thy beauty see,
Thy countenance behold:
Thy rays of grace, fixed in my face,
More rich than massy gold.

Let royal robes of praise,
And righteousness adorn me,
Which may me bring, before the King,
How ever mortals scorn me.

Let treasures of thy grace,
A portion rich endow me;
In lasting bags, though here in rags,
Men scarce a bit allow me.

If comeliness I want,
Thy beauty may I have;
I shall be fair, beyond compare,
Though crippled to my grave.

And if above it all,
To Christ I married be;
My living springs, Oh King of kings,
Will still run fresh in thee.

> *Upon a Bible sent as a token to a young virgin, wherein the worth*
> *of the holy Scripture is minded.*[3]

While I was musing what was best,
unto your hands to send:
That of your soul's eternal rest,
my care I might commend:
The Holy Scriptures I bethought,
oft tendering to your heart,
That your affections might be brought,
to choose the better part.

There you may read what guilt of sin,
into the world you brought?
And since what filthiness hath been,
in word, in deed, in thought:
How God's long-suffering, sins have pressed,
as sheaves do press a cart;
And nothing else can make you blessed,
but Mary's better part.

That God hath holy jealous eyes,
the Scriptures do unfold;
By which heart-secrets he espies,
yet cannot sin behold.
Through shades of death, and darkest night,
these piercing beams do dart;
He looks on nothing with delight,
but on that better part.

With flaming fire you also read,
a judgment day design'd,
Where every idle thought and deed,
Must righteous sentence find.
These kings stand naked, death hath hurl'd
their robes and crowns apart;

---

3. Ibid., 31–33.

Then, but too late, they'll give the world
for Mary's better part.

Then to have Jesus Christ ones own,
will be admired grace;
To stand with boldness at the throne,
and see the Father's face.
To sit on thrones, when Christ shall say,
Ye wicked ones depart.
But come ye blessed in my day,
ye chose the better part.

The tenders of his grace so rich,
here Jesus doth display.
He scarlet-sinners doth beseech,
his Gospel to obey:
To let sins fettered captives free,
and heal the broken heart:
He begs them on his bended knee,
to choose the better part.

Deep myst'ries of eternal love,
hid from the saints of old;
To babes and sucklings from above,
these Scriptures do unfold:
Not in the words of frothy wits,
or humane terms of art;
But such simplicity as fits,
The Spirit's better part.

The glory of the Father's face,
the burning Law declares:
The beauty of Christ's precious grace,
the Gospel here prepares,
Both grace and glory here unite,
to heal sins deadly smart.
The Spirit, and the Bride invite,
to choose this better part.

The blessed truths display'd herein,
all your dear pleasures make;
Its sharp rebukes of every sin,
as healing balsam take.
For though convictions to the flesh,
so bitter seem and tart;
Yet is their issue to refresh,
and heal the better part.

Oh! then upon this Word of Truth,
place high and great esteem:
This point of wisdom learn in youth,
your precious time redeem.
To know Christ's from a stranger's voice,
account the highest art;
Your richest treasure is your choice
of Mary's better part.

A Poetical Meditation,
wherein the usefulness, excellency, and several perfections of the holy
Scriptures are briefly hinted, perform'd by J. C. but turn'd into more familiar
verse for the use of children,
by Abr. Chear.[4]

Among thy glorious gifts;
Lord thou thy Word hast given,
Precious and pure, sweet, holy, sure,
To guide me hence to heaven.

Here I abound with straits,
Wants and necessities,
There I have store, heaped, running ore,
With plenteous rich supplies.

Temptations here abound,
With terrors, dangers, fears,
These petty hells thy Word expels,
And all my passage clears.

When Satan fiercely shoots,
His fiery darts at me;
Then Lord, thy Word, is shield and sword,
Me saves and makes them flee.

The present world commends,
Its objects fresh and fair;
But yet thy Word doth that afford,
Which proves more precious ware.

When fleshly lusts entice,
To their alluring pleasure;
To rare delights thy Word invites,
More choice in weight and measure.

---

4. Ibid., 34–38.

The errors of the times;
Their cheating wares display;
But Scripture says, shun error's ways.
My rule shall guide your way.

When by the Tempter's wiles,
I tempted am to sin;
By thy Word's art, hid in my heart,
Both field and prize I win.

Nay though I soiled be,
And sin defile my soul,
Thy Word can cleanse these noisome dens,
And sin's best strength control.

An unbelieving heart,
Do I till now inherit:
Lord, thy Word hath pow'r to work faith,
By thy most Holy Spirit.

If this be my disease,
An hard and stony heart;
Thy Word thus deals, first kills, then heals,
And cures me by this smart.
Will not my frozen heart,
With Gospel grace comply;
Thy royal Law, this heart can thaw,
And cause a weeping eye.

Doth lofty towering thoughts,
Puff up my tempted breast;
Thy word brings low, the proudest foe,
Less makes me than the least.

Do muttering thoughts arise,
Grudge, murmur, or repine;
Thy rod and Word, teach patience, Lord,
And still these thoughts of mine.

Am I tongue-ti'd in prayer,
And know not what to say:
Thy Word inspires, praying desires,
Tells how and what to pray.

When like a lost sheep I
In darkness err and stray:
Thy word's a light, most clear and bright,
And guides me in my way.

A simple fool I be,
And destitute of eyes;
Thy word's a rule, master, and school,
To make its scholars wise.

I see my self undone,
Distressed, naked, poor,
Thy words enfold a mind of gold,
Rich pearls, and precious store.

By sinful nature I
And God are still at odds,
Thy Word my soul converteth whole,
From Satan's will to God's.

Do troubles from without.
And floods of inward grief
My soul torment? Thy Word is lent,
With joy and soul relief.

Or, is my soul perplexed,
With reasonings, doubts, and fears,
Thy Word of grace, resolves the case,
My cloudy judgment clears.

Or, do despairing thoughts,
My tempted soul o'rtake?
Thy word doth give, me hopes to live,
For Christ my Saviour's sake.

Waiting on the Spirit of Promise

When floods and multitudes
Of troubled thoughts me press;
I call to mind, thy word, and find,
Its joys my soul refresh.

Though in this vale of tears
I thirst, faint, hunger, pine;
Thy word me feeds, in these my ne[eds]
Its bread, and milk, and wine.

Or, am I weakened out,
And cannot walk alone;
Thy word then is strength to my knees,
And staff to lean upon.

And though in scorn and pain,
Forsook, and poor I be,
Thy word alone, hath all in one,
Health, wealth, friends, all to me,

Thus though my pained soul
Be sick, and wounded sore,
With grievous sin, which doth begin,
To fester more and more.

Thy word directs me where,
My healing may be had,
And doth me guide, to Christ's pierc'd side,
For Balm of Gilead.

Nay, though no life at all,
Nor quickening there remain;
Thy word is good, and living food,
Which fetcheth life again.

And if I would desire,
A life that lasts for ever;
The Scripture shows, whence water flows,
To drink and perish never.

Blessed be the Lord my God,
Who evermore provides,
And filleth full, my empty soul,
With food that still abides.

My soul! O bless the Lord,
Who bounteously hath given,
Strength, light, guide, way, lest thou shouldst stray,
In this thy way to heaven.

This Holy Book of God,
These sentences, these lines;
Each word and letter, to me are better,
Than pearls and golden mines.

'Tis heaven it self transcrib'd,
And glory lively pen'd;
God's truth, no doubt was, copied out,
When he this gift did send.

Its truth brought forth to light;
God did hereby intend,
Man's word should fall, heaven, earth, and all,
But this should never end.

Dear soul, admiring stand,
At that blessed hand and quill;
That did produce, for sinners use.
Th'eternal sovereign will.

Astonished admire,
The Author too; and when
Thou canst not raise, sufficient praise,
With wondering say, Amen.

To my cousin W.L.[5]

Dear child, although my Father's will
in prison me hath bound;
Through uprightness, and patience still,
my comforts here are found.
The presence of a gracious God,
doth this a palace make;
It makes the bitter of the rod,
be sweet for Jesus' sake.
But Oh! when guilt brings any here,
in fetters to be bound;
Because of God they had no fear,
but were in evil found:
To such it is a dreadful place,
here guilt to judgment binds them;
Where if they don't repent apace,
Death, wrath, and vengeance finds them.
Of you, dear child, with carefulness,
my heart hath many a thought;
Least you though youthful wantonness,
to greater sins be brought:
And so by adding sin to sin,
you waste your time and strength;
And when your judgment doth begin,
in vain you mourn at length.
I charge you then, in any sort,
your great Creator mind;
Spend not your youthful days in sport,
that cannot be regain'd.
Avoid those rude and wicked boys,
that make a mock of sin;
Love not their plays, and sinful toys,
to fear the Lord begin.
Keep close to school, read Scriptures oft,
in private learn to pray;
Your Gospel-grounds keep still in thought,

---

5. Ibid., 41–42.

your parents both obey.
Your brethren love, and teach them good,
a Christian learn to be;
Then God will give you clothes and food,
and you'll be dear to me.

Verses affixed to the wall of the prison, at the Guild-hall in Plymouth: where A. C. was detained a month, and thence sent to the Island, the 27th. Sept. 1665.[6]

Nigh four years since, sent out from hence,
To Exon Goal was I,[7]
but special grace in three months' space,
wrought out my liberty.
Till Bartholomew in sixty two,[8]
that freedom did remain;
Then without bail to Exon jail,
I hurried was again.
Where having lain, as do the slain,
'mong dead men wholly free;
Full three years' space, my native place,
By leave I come to see.
And thought not then, I here again,
a month's restraint should find,
Since, to my den, cast out from men,
I'm during life design'd.
But since my lines the Lord assigns,
In such a lot to be,
I kiss the rod, confess, my God
deals faithfully with me.
My charged crime, in his due time,
He fully will decide,
And until then, forgiving men,
In peace with him I bide.

---

6. Ibid., 86–87.
7. "Exon" is another spelling for "Exeter."
8. St. Bartholomew's Day, 1662.

On the beginning of his recovering from a great sickness,
on the Island of Plymouth.[9]

To his truly Sacred Majesty, the High and Mighty Potentate, King of kings, and Lord of lords, Prince of Life and peace, Heir of all things, and Head over all to the Church.

    The humble prostrature, and thankful acknowledgment, of a poor prisoner of hope, whose life upon all accompts hath been marvelously preserved, and delivered with a great salvation from the pit of corruption.

Most glorious Sovereign to thy feet is brought,
The trembling offspring of a contrite thought
By a poor captive who attempts to raise,
An Eben-ezer to his Saviour's praise.
A lasting pillar as in conscience bound,
In due remembrance of choice favours found;
With grace to succour in a needful hour,
From death's dominion, and the Tempter's power.
But when thy worm reflects what can it bring,
Comporting with the grandeur of a king;
Of such bright majesty, as angels must
Their faces veil before, shall sinful dust
Have bold access, and kind acceptance meet,
For self and service at thy burning feet?
May hair, badgers-skin, a widow's mite,
From willing minds, find favour in thy sight;
A pair of pigeons, or a turtle dove,
Find kind construction from the God of love?
Is there more over-laid by the supply,
To help such weakness in infirmity?
A costly covering doth thy grace provide,
Their blemishes to veil, their spots to hide,
Who from their sense of need and duty bring
Their lowly homage to their lofty King?
On such encouragements here trembling stands,
A contrite waiter though with empty hands.

    9. Cheare and Jessey, *Looking-Glass*, 87–89. The Island of Plymouth was also known as Drake's Island.

Whose bag and basket speak him to become,
More like a beggar than a bringer home,
Who though he aims and longs in this address,
His utmost obligations to express,
To charge his conscience, and discharge his vow,
Abandon other lords, to Jesus bow;
Yet finds in all, that, void of royal aid,
Naught worthy of thee can be thought or said.
Apart from Christ the best attempts (alas,)
Are tinkling cymbals and as sounding brass,
Such stately structures prove but wood and hay.
I'th test and contest of that burning day,
These dear experiments so often tri'd;
All boasting confidence from flesh must hide.
Of self-sufficiency in best attire,
To form that work, or breathe but that desire,
Or think that thought, that can in justice claim,
One heavenly aspect on its act or aim.
What then remains, thy worm must prostrate fall,
While sentence from thy presence past on all,
Which self hath gloried in, or flesh hath gain'd,
With whatsoer'e to Adam appertain'd,
His wisdom, will, his power, delight, desire,
Or what his art, or industry acquire;
His noblest faculties, acutest parts,
His liberal sciences or rarest arts.
Nay his best righteousness, his all in all,
Must be resign'd, surrendered, lest to fall,
Be sentenc'd, crucified, dispoil'd, disgrac'd,
And at the feet of conquering Jesus plac'd;
That on its ruins, Gospel-grace may rear
A living pillar, thy new name to bear.

Words in Season:

From that late Worthy Sufferer, and Servant of the Lord Jesus, an able Minister of the *New-Testament*, according to that Character, 2 *Cor.* 6. 4, 5, &c.

Mr. *Abraham Cheare.*

VIZ.

I. Faith's Conquest, over the Tortures and Tenders of an Hour of Temptation, on *Heb.* 11. 35.

II. The Embalming of a Dead Cause, on *Mark* 14. 8.

III. Remarkable Discourses on his Dying-Bed, with Copies and Extracts of Letters, on several occasions.

Useful for those, whose Hearts are engaged to serve the Will of God, in this Generation.

London, Printed for *Nathan Brookes*, in *Bartholomew-Close*, 1668.

7

Abraham Cheare, *Words in Season*

His Final Words[1]

A FRIEND GIVING HIM some emulsion to drink, he drank and said, "All passages are clear, between stomach and belly, head and heart, and that and heaven, blessed be God."

A friend then asking him if he had any thing to say to them in the family with him, in case the Lord should call him from them? He replied, "I desire the blessing of the God of Heaven may be upon you, and a full reward from him be ministered to you for all the labour of love you have shewed to me for the Lord's sake; and I beseech you continue steadfast in the faith and testimony to Christ and his concerns, who is as worthy as ever, notwithstanding all the reproach cast on him and them; and I desire earnestly you will take heed of being offended at Him, his Word, works, or ways, but be careful to be found in his paths, as even you hope to have help, to stand before him with peace and comfort at his appearing."

He further said, "Christ had a poor remnant yet left, that he was persuaded should be helped to stand, and no more to be afraid of the worst that men can do, than he, through grace, was now afraid of what death could do to him." And said, "Though I may be rolled into my dust, yet there is a promised approaching glory, that God will most certainly bring forth out of all these great deeps, with which we are now encompassed, though (says he) it may be you also may not live to see it, but to die in the faith of it will be enough; and the Lord grant you may not stagger, and that no cloud

---

1. Cheare, *Words in Season*, 175–212 *passim*. For extensive selections of *Words in Season*, see also Nicholson, *Authentic Records*, 17–53.

may be upon your testimony to God, nor (unless clouds be good for you) upon your interest in him."

And as to the church at Plymouth, he said, he had oft, since his sickness, on his bed, begg'd of God, that the Lord the God of the spirits of all flesh, would send a man over that church, a man whom he should choose, to go in and out before them, to feed them, that so the Lord's poor flock be not utterly scattered by those that carry or keep them captive (Numbers 27 he referred to).

And further said to a friend then present, "I desire you, if God by his Providence or otherwise, shall hereafter speak any such thing to you, though but in a whisper, you would not despise or neglect it, but look on it as the call of God to you, and obey it accordingly . . ."

After this discourse ended, he further said, he had been a poor staggering vain creature, and since the time he came to this place, and the Lord gave a little recovery, he had not so improved it as became him; he earnestly wished he could write a little, that he might leave a witness against it. Saying also, "Ah! I have many things in short-hand, that none can read but my self, by which means they will be lost."

Then added, "I have a poor sister, an honest affectionate soul, who I desire you will do what you can to comfort, support and strengthen, according to that counsel (1 Thessalonians 5:14), 'Now we exhort you brethren, warn them that are unruly, comfort the feeble-minded, support the weak, be patient towards all men.'" And desired we would sometimes speak a word in season to her. And further said, as to the church in Plymouth, wherein he had laboured, he designed to serve the Lord in it, and to gather souls to Christ; and had now the witness of a good conscience in that matter, that he had not willfully omitted, or dealt negligently in that work in the main of it, as opportunity presented; and blessed the Lord, that since his imprisonment, he had heard of six or seven of that Church, that had gone triumphing to heaven before him.

Then speaking of Christians sufferings, he minded that word (1 Peter 4:16), 'Yet if any man suffer as a Christian, etc.' He minded what a blessed thing it was to suffer as a Christian, viz. To begin, hold on, hold out, and at last come off as a Christian; It was a great word and work, and speaking of his pains he had on his outward-man, yet blessed God, There was no sorrow added, nor no sting in them, that was stuck in the sides of Christ, blessed be his Name.

A friend asking how he did? "Never better in my life (said he) blessed be God."

One asked him whether he would have any cordial? He said, "Yes, may it be an instrument on God's behalf to recover a little strength before I go hence, and be seen no more, to speak yet a word for God, else take me of no more cordials, for I drink full draughts." One giving him a little, he drank and said, "I am made to drink of the best spiced wine, the wine of the pomegranate; his love is better than wine; I am drinking of a vineyard, not a drop of red wine blessed be God: the day I think is come, I shall be led to the Fountain of Living Water, and shall hunger nor thirst no more;" And added, "The wine that is red might have been my portion, even fire and brimstone, and an horrible tempest, might have been the portion of my cup..."

His sister desired to know how he was satisfied as to his coming hither, she having been the occasion as she judged of his coming from Exon [Exeter] to Plymouth, and consequently of his coming hither; He answered, "Very well satisfied, all have been steps of divine ordering; I would not have come from Exon, might I have had my own will; I would not have stayed in Plymouth, a'ter I had preached once, but God would have me stay; I would not have come to this place, after my time of suffering was out in the Town-Hall at Plymouth, if I might have had my own will; but God would bring me hither, and blessed be the Lord that let me not have my own will, blessed be God that brought me here, and blessed me here, with desirable company and mercies, concerning which we have had occasions and seasons to speak well of God together; yea, since I have been brought here, and sick here, yet the steps of God have been in great wisdom with me, and the bottom of them all paved with love, in the main of his goings in these dark and heavy strokes; I say, in the main of them they have been attended with peace to my soul; I have had old wine, or new, afforded still; sometimes he hath said the old is better, and hath made ancient experiences of his love, sweet to me, yet not always alike clear; sometimes he hath seen good to cut short within and without, and this last trial, to deal plainly, came on in somewhat a cloud, at its entrance I was somewhat stupid, thinking no more in it than ordinary; but I was at last awakened by the Lord to think that this might be a long and close trial, and though he let me see the anchor dropped within the vail, yet had I not that freshness of evidence, till within a few days last past, when he called up my spirit to a close search, in a night or two, though I said but little of it, but he graciously issued that matter in a token of good, that whether I live or die, I hope I shall wear to his praise, while I have my being; so that thus 'tis with me now, Christ is lovely to me in all the afflictions I have met with, in all I have seen and suffered: wherefore rejoice with me, O my friends, let us rejoice and bless the name of the Lord together that hath dealt well with me; and do not I beseech you disgrace the throne of his glory, because of me or this fleshly state that must be taken from you. Murmur not I pray ye, that yet you see not Saviours come up upon Mount Zion. The reserve of Spirit is with him, and the Lord hath many children to bring in, besides those that are brought, that shall be brought in by virtue of fresh anointing, so as they shall be known to be children of his that he hath blessed: And as I desire you would not weep for me, so not inordinately for your selves neither; adhere to Christ, and fear none of those things ye shall suffer. I have no deep insight into deep mysteries; but this I believe God is a-rising to do some great thing in the world for Sion's sake, and though it be hard for us to lose our chariots and horsemen, some by apostasy, some by death, some by scattering, yet when the gathering time shall be, it will be no grief, nor sorrow of heart to behold the way of God's working in all these things, when we shall say he hath done all things well.

There are many signs upon us, that prognostic great things near at the doors, though I dare not say I know much distinctly as to times, means, and methods, only be assured not one jot or tittle of all God hath spoke shall fail, though our interpretations of them may fail.

If any ask how it stood with me, as to these things at this season, tell them, 'If I die, I die in as full assurance that God will give reviving to his poor despised cause and interest, as I do believe the resurrection of this body, and that I know both the one and the other are founded on such a word as shall stand as mountains of brass.' And advise them also, to take heed how they wait on men's indulgence, so much talked of, but let their faith stand in the wisdom, power, and faithfulness of God, and their prayers be directed more that way, endeavouring to make religion their business; yet if any shall lean to such a deceitful bow, be not you dismayed or discouraged at it, but hold on your way, that shall be strength to you..."

And further said, He had had his reflections, and he thought some injections also, that day of his neglects of service for the Lord, that he might better have improved in times past, though in the main, "the testimony I have born to Christ, in my day, is a quieting, comforting consideration, through the blood of Christ, though not the bottoming consideration, on which my peace is built, yet 'tis of great use, in a secondary sort, at such a season; and I mention it to you, that you may do much, suffer much, shrink not, nor neglect no work for God; it will be no grief of heart to any that have spent, and been spent, for God, his name and interest for days to come."

Being very ill, and, in the apprehensions of those about him, like to leave them, he was asked, Had he any further word to them, or any of the Lord's people, before he left them. To which he answered, "I have spoken to you and them already the whole counsel of God, according to what I have received, and was under no temptation, to keep back any thing through fraud; I cannot now speak much, and if I could, unless the great Remembrancer set home with power and efficacy, what is spoken upon our minds and spirits, it will signify but little; and to add many words, would be but a vanity: but for you, and them, and all saints, I pray that you may abide with God, and never be ashamed or tempted with fear or cowardice, or unbecoming compliances with base earthly worldly interests to let go your holdfast on any truth you have professed, as truth is in Jesus.

I have delivered to that poor church I appertain unto, the doctrine of a free Gospel of grace, wherein a foundation is laid in the blood of Jesus, of peace with God through him, and they also, have with hands lift up to the most High, professedly accepted that graced tendered to them; and I being, I think, about to leave earth, and to go to my Father, and give an account of my stewardship therein; I do go in full assurance that it is the true grace of God wherein they stand; and I do lay it before them, with the utmost ability such a poor worm as I can do, that they be not by doctrine, word, nor spirit, soon shaken from their steadfastness, hither or thither, for life or salvation, but as they have been taught."

He farther said, "I also have been engaged in a witness to the royal sovereignty of Christ in his institutions, against the inventions of men opposed thereunto; which testimony hath been born up against blindness and ignorance, in a poor dark world that lies in ignorance and wickedness; and their testimony in fellowship with this of mine, hath flourished in former days, under those more promising propitious prospects we were then encompassed and encouraged with, it had then by them and others, Hosannas ascribed to it; but since God hath seen good to try this testimony; and spirits of such as profess it with a day of adversity, that many looked not for, and they have hereby been tempted basely and unworthily to throw away the shield, as if it never had been anointed; the thoughts whereof hath many times almost broken my heart in pieces: But let all such know, I go away in this firm persuasion, as to the things we have together professed as aforesaid, that they are the true sayings of God, and that such as in this hour of temptation have deserted their profession of them, God will meet with all such if he love them, to awaken and recover them from such paths and postures of back-sliding, or else to make them know, to their shame, and confusion of face, that they have dealt dishonourably with Christ and his concerns, and dangerously with their own souls; which I desire they may find mercy to repent unfeignedly of, before it be too late…"

"I have mentioned heretofore to you, and others, what it was, and how it was, the Lord had begot and carried on in me; and thought it had been above questions, yet had I some doubts and fears renewed of a very ancient date, about, if not above thirty years ago, with many miscarriages since to promote the same matter; and this coming in a time of such weakness, and when by the working of my spleen, which sent up dark and disturbing vapours, clouding my imagination, and made sore work within; but the Lord made me see much of my own fleshly gloryings, as also others in me, and in my flesh, which God would take down in this day of trial, when every ones work must be tried of what sort it is, even by fire; and truly I was made to see to my shame, much hypocrisy and formality in my converse with the Lord in one respect or other, and that the practical part of religion I had yet arrived to little acquaintance with, to what I had in days past; but this brought me in the issue to see, that I was, what I was, that was good, only by grace, and no room for flesh to glory, but was brought through grace to experience this truth, that when I am weak, then am I strong; and that however it be, yet the Lord forgetteth not his poor, nor despiseth not his prisoners; this is a brief account of the way God led me in, in this matter, and hath so issued it, that I trust through grace, I shall yet come to lay down my weary head and heart in the peace of God's speaking, that will keep and carry me to the end."

Letters

To a friend, long kept close prisoner, under hard circumstances, and greater threatenings.[1]

Everlasting joy upon your head, while sorrow and sighing flee away.[2]

Beloved, and honoured by and for the Lord!

This morning, having obtained that mercy from the Lord, of reading a character of your heart drawn by your own hand, wherewithal I and others were not a little refreshed, and a safe hand presenting for the conveyance of this to you, which I hope may reach you, I thought my self providentially called and concerned to give you a testimony of my joy in the grace of Christ, which is engaged hitherto to uphold you with everlasting arms, that neither the strength nor length of your suffering is such to you, as is accompted otherwise by you than right, and but for a moment, being laid on the balance with the glory that is ready to be revealed in us. In this way of reckoning, while our eye is kept on invisible and eternal weights of glory, realizing and impropriating them, crowns of thorns are more easy and less dishonourable than at a distance they seem to be, or than we sense and apprehend them, while we are reasoning after the flesh. Weights indeed they have and are, and such as make the oppressed many times to groan earnestly, none for the present being joyous but grievous, and are tenderly thought upon by him, who in all their afflictions is afflicted, the Angel of whose presence also is with them; but we know the end of the Lord, and his rest shall be glorious, when his indignation ceaseth in their destruction;

---

1. Cheare, *Words in Season*, 243–46.
2. Isa 35:10.

but he rests in his love, and there also shall make the weary to rest. I judge my self some-way rebuked from above, and untaught what and how to pray as I ought, if in any prayer of mine I forget the sons of your noble order, and especially in seeking what you desire; namely, that you through the greatness of faith may enter into rest, and at this time of day, while he hath taken business out of your hand, he may the more abundantly acquaint and refresh you with that dismission to rest, as may secure you until the indignation be over-past. You know his privilege, who (Jeremiah 36:5) though he was shut up, that he could not walk abroad about his Lord's business, was nevertheless hid there by the Lord; when the courtiers did purpose to take him, (verse 26) But if in the Father's counsel it appear best, that out of these store-houses he bring more of his precious boxes of ointment to be poured out upon the present funerals of the cause he is concerned in, I make no question but the savour thereof will commend it self all the virgins in this and other generations, and they shall have robes and rest, till they stand again in their lot at the end of days; and who believing and loving Jesus Christ in truth, would not put on his filthy garments, in expectation of such change of raiment?

As for my part, my Father graciously indulgeth me, and the lambs here, giving us an undeserved covert (of which no reason can be given) everywhere Satan's seat is, while other flocks are dispersed and scattered. Near about us, by my last I acquainted, that some from our neighbouring parts, are sent to that place of ancient experience, where they have a stock of prayers and presence to begin upon: they begin on straw, as learning to endure hardness as good soldiers; the Lord make that word good to them, which often hath been in that place sweet to me (Exodus 23:25) and at length (Ecclesiastes 4:14) expect daily the same lot, in the Lord's with-holding his hand from which, I fear nothing more than a spirit apt to do as Agag (1 Samuel 15:32) putting off the evil day, the least sun-shine brought forth a manifestation, that notwithstanding the ruin of his nation, and danger of himself, he was not mortified to the delicacy of his life; nor had escaped (though he thought he had waved) the bitterness of his death.

I need your prayers and precious exhortations, tending to prevent slumber, that I be not taken at unawares. The Lord keep fresh and manifest before your eyes and mine, the Captain of our salvation, not only as a leading pattern, but as a life-giving principle, on which having our minds stayed, we may still be trusting in him, as kept in peace upon peace there, with true respects to all your family,

    Rests,
    Yours, in the love of Jesus.
    26th 4th month, 62.[3]

---

3. The dating here is according to the Julian calendar, known as the Old Style, in which the year began on March 25. March was reckoned the first month, so the fourth month is June. So the date here is 26 June 1662.

His judgment about continuing, or, forbearing assemblies to worship the Lord.[4]

Strength and beauty, as is in the sanctuary.[5]

Beloved in the Lord!
I thought it best, while it is yet day, and opportunity offers, that we attempt to make improvement so, as may mutually tend to the strengthening each others faith and love in Christ Jesus, with such intimations of occurrences as may direct to suitable sympathy and supplication, as the interest of the Lord may require in its present circumstances, at their hands, who have learned to approve themselves as true Sionists. This place affords little, save the continued series of divine goodness holding our souls in life, and not suffering our feet to be moved, where he with-holds not the tokens of his Fatherly care and provision to supply all our wants both outwardly and within, to shew that he is God our Rock, and no unrighteousness is with him.[6]

We had rumours of being this week brought before the Deputy Lieutenant, but that came to nothing. Fear and fury fills many men's hands with work of their own occasioning; so doth he make their own tongue fall upon themselves; the righteous shall see it and flee away; and all men shall see and consider the works of God, for they shall wisely consider his doing.

They at our Island I hear are well and cheerful, but free access to them is denied, nothing else can be expected as times and jealousies are; yet heaven is open still. David could form a song in the cave when his faith reached to this assurance, "He shall send from heaven and save me."[7] Earth was block'd up, but heaven was open still. And as long as heaven holds, he had no ground to mistrust a want of the promises accomplishment to the uttermost. Many thoughts of heart have exercised us as well in groans at the throne as in other sad conferences among our selves at the reasonings and resolves of your strong men, who by drawing away the shoulder from the yoke, and their hand from the plough, wherein they seemed so well skilled and blessed formerly, have given way to the ceasing of their work in a time when their faith and love to Christ is brought to its trial; and that any poor

---

4. Cheare, *Words in Season*, 246–248.
5. Ps 96:6.
6. Ps 92:15.
7. Ps 57:3.

souls should interpose with their lives in their hands, to bear up the name of Christ, and to preserve a nail in his house; in their absence it serves to signify, that there is something of reality in that promise, "The last shall be first, and the first last."[8] And touching your question, "What ground a church hath, in times of persecution, to appear publicly?" If by publicly be meant only so far knowingly as wherein (with the best prudence and caution used as their case stands) they may most effectually answer the ends of mutual edification, and hold up the glory of Christ in the practice of his institutions; It's so far from being a question, "What grounds they have to meet?" as we know not what grounds can well be held up to the contrary, by any who pretend to so much profession, as that any part of the instituted will of God is worth the suffering for, or that Christ is worth the following in Gospel-precepts, when the obedience of saints therein is to be tried as by fire. If you be pleased to single out any reasons that can pretend to satisfy conscience, guided by the mind of God in Scripture, they may have an examination.

Rests,
Yours, many ways obliged.
20th 7th month, 62. [9]

---

8. Matt 20:16.
9. That is, 20 September 1662. See above, p. 93, n.3.

To a friend released out of prison.[10]

Wisdom and understanding exceeding much and largeness of heart like the sand of the sea.

Precious and Beloved!
I have my longings to know how it fareth with your soul, now you are under the advantage of gathering up at liberty the diffused light and anointing that is dropped with such variety in the Body of Christ especially in your city, whither, I observe it is the aim of most of the choice persons up and down, who either are driven, or disengaged from necessary attendance in their country stations, to make haste, promising themselves greater liberty and enjoyment there than ordinarily here can be expected. In respect whereof I have been sometimes conceiting that it is a place, and puts into a capacity for believers to make the most rare extracts, and pick out the choicest notions and assistances of anywhere in the world; which thoughts are easily attended with such temptations, Oh! that I had the wings of a dove, I would flee far away from this stormy wind and tempest, I would see that goodly mountain and Lebanon.[11] But then I am as often checked with this reproof, "He that increaseth knowledge, increaseth sorrow"; these creaturely engagements may render a man the more prudent and rational; it's many to one if they make him more serious, spiritual, evangelical.[12] It may be easy to get the mind fraughted with noise, news, notions; but to get the heart established with grace, drawn into a more substantial and experimental communion with Jesus Christ, according to the tenor of the New-Covenant, and in the grace and truth thereof; this is not so easy to be found and maintained, without extraordinary watch and diligence. These words of wisdom, may be more heard in quiet, and to better purpose and improvement, than in the out-cry of him that ruleth among fools. Soul-searching, heart-preparing, sin-mortifying work, may have more advantage from the retirement of a nasty prison, than (unless abundance of grace be ministered) from being left to walk in a large place, especially if with a large principle of liberty to touch withal, but being laid in Gospel-bonds under the instituted charge of none. In these respects (my much valued in the Lord!) I have not only had

---

10. Cheare, *Words in Season*, 251–53.
11. Ps 55:6; Deut 3:25.
12. Eccl 1:18.

some trials of my own soul, while I have been representing things to my self in such a figure; and also seen the woeful issues thereof on some others who have fallen under my short-sighted observation; but have withal had many a thought of you, since you have been (in an outward respect) as a hind let loose; I will not say I have had hints of any tamperings with you, but only, that it is marvelous if you have not, which doth and will so much the more magnify grace in your being preserved in Christ Jesus, steadfast in the faith, fervent in the Spirit, lively and active in the ways of God, growing up more into Christ which is our Head, and being more publicly diffused by a largeness of Spirit in all the members. This, all this I hope, pray, and shall to my utmost endeavour, may be found remaining and increasing in you, according to the form of sound words, the pattern of them who first trusted in Christ, worthy of all the grace you have received, and testimony you have born hitherto in doing and suffering, and worthy of the blessed hope, of the resurrection of the Lord's cause, and the approaching of his promised glory. In a fellowship in this earnest expectation and endeavour, you have the prayers of all our little family, but especially and particularly of,

Your wonted, and constant soul-friend.

26th 6th month, 63.[13]

---

13. That is, 26 August 1663. See above, p. 93, n.3.

To a friend, who, after some retirement, was returning to pursue his calling in affairs of this world.[14]

The Lord be your shade, on your right-hand.[15]

My very dear brother!

I perceive you are applying your self to something men call, business in the world; and I have comfortable hopes, that you have studied ere this hour that lesson, "Finally brethren, the time is short, it remaineth, &c. For the fashion of this world passeth away."[16] Oh my dear brother! My soul is afflicted to observe the over-greedy engagement of many (whom I love and honour for their former eminency) plunging themselves into business, and there even drowning themselves in ruin and perdition; losing the savour of their spirits, the intimacy of their communion with Christ in the Spirit, and so grow dry, careless, prudent, fearful, omissive, what not? till there is hardly left so much as the uniform appearance of a soul, that hath been the seat of such glorious discoveries and enjoyments as men have readily spoke of formerly. It may well be asked of many now, as the Apostle, "Where is the blessedness ye spoke of?"[17] Men discourse of their primitive applications of truth, and to it speak much and frequently of blessedness in the things of the Gospel; it was blessed praying, and blessed hearing, and blessed meeting, and blessed meditating; because in all these they sought after, and partook of blessedness! But where is that now? There is somewhat of praying, and preaching, &c. but where is the blessedness of all these? Is it not very much departed, and what may be the cause? Is it not much from hence? Men are gone deep into the spirit of the world, and are grown carnal, of the earth earthy, and savouring of the earth, and thereby losing their love, zeal, faithfulness, insensibly, but very dangerously. I hope better things of you,

---

14. Cheare, *Words in Season*, 261–62.
15. Ps 121:5.
16. 1 Cor 7:29, 31.
17. Gal 4:15.

and that you both do and will watch your own spirit, and stir up others to take great heed to their spirits, that they deal not treacherously.

Yours,
7th 3rd month, 64.[18]

---

18. That is, 7 May 1664. See above, p. 93, n.3.

To a friend, upon the release of some, who had been divers years imprisoned.[19]

Dear Friend!

I am glad if those friends come safe on shore; it there be nothing of a witness to be look'd at in such a lot, it's good to get to land with all speed: but if there be any thing of our being set, for the defence (or apology) of the Gospel (Philippians 1:17) though but in the smallest point of it, it may be very hazardous shifting places (Acts 27:31, 1 Samuel 22:23, 1 Corinthians 9:15–16). If God look for a man in the gap, though but to defend a piece of barley (1 Chronicles 11:13–14) or though but of lentils (2 Samuel 23:11–12). If it be any part of the heritage of Israel; it will not be easy answering that question, when found in a way of escaping, "What dost thou here Eliah?"[20] It needs great care and caution to come out of Egypt well leavened, when the most are making haste, that they may not die in the pit. When will that Roman greatness be out-shone by Christian nobility of spirit? (Acts 16:37)

Yours.

30th of the 9th mon. 67.[21]

---

19. Cheare, *Words in Season*, 286.
20. 1 Kgs 19:13.
21. That is, 30 November 1667. See above, p. 93, n.3.

Bibliography

Anderson, Philip J. "A Fifth Monarchist Appeal and the Response of an Independent Church of Canterbury, 1653." *The Baptist Quarterly* 33/2 (April 1989) 72–80.
Baxter, Richard. *The Life of Faith.* Vol. 12 of *The Practical Works of the Rev. Richard Baxter*, edited by William Orme. London: James Duncan, 1830.
Bellamy, Richard. *The Leper Cleansed.* London: Francis Eglesfield, 1657.
Bennet, Robert. "Guide to the Papers of Robert Bennet, 1603-1678." Folger Shakespeare Library. Washington, DC: 1603–1678. http://titania.folger.edu/findingaids/dfobennet.xml.
Binmore, J. W. *The History of the Baptist Church, Dartmouth.* Dartmouth, UK: Tozer, 1950.
Bosworth, F. "The Sufferings of the Early Baptists in Devon." *Bible Christian Magazine* 11 (1875) 528.
Briggs, J. H. Y., ed. *Faith, Heritage and Witness.* London: Baptist Historical Society, 1987.
Brook, Benjamin. *The Lives of the Puritans.* Vol. 3. London: J. Black, 1813.
Capp, Bernard. "*A Door of Hope* Re-Opened: The Fifth Monarchy, King Charles and King Jesus." *Journal of Religious History* 32/1 (2008) 16–30.
―――. *The Fifth Monarchy Men.* London: Faber, 1972.
Cheare, Abraham. *Words in Season.* London: Nathan Brookes, 1668.
Cheare, Abraham, et al. *Sighs for Sion.* London: Livewel Chapman, 1657.
Cheare, Abraham, and Henry Jessey. *A Looking-Glass for Children.* 3rd ed. London: Robert Boulter, 1673.
Cheare, Abraham, and Robert Steed. *A Plain Discovery of the Unrighteous Judge and False Accuser.* London: Henry Mortlock, 1658.
Cramp, J. M. *Baptist History: From the Foundation of the Christian Church to the Present Time.* London: E. Stock, 1871.
Crosby, Thomas. *The History of the English Baptists.* Vol. 1. London: John Robinson, 1740.
Durso, Keith E. *No Armor For the Back: Baptist Prison Writings, 1600s–1700s.* Macon, GA: Mercer University Press, 2007.
F. A. [pseud.]. *A Letter from a Gentleman in Grayes-Inn, to a Justice of the Peace in the Countrey.* N.p., 1662.
Foster, John C. "Early Baptist Writers of Verse." *Transactions of the Baptist Historical Society* 3/2 (October 1912) 95–110.
Gill, Crispin. *Plymouth: A New History.* Tiverton, UK: Devon, 1993.
Greenslade, J. "The Origin of the Baptists in Plymouth." *The Earthen Vessel and Christian Record and Review* 13 (December 1, 1857) 286–88.

Hastings, F. G. "A Pilgrimage to Drake's Island." *The Baptist Quarterly* 7/7 (July 1935) 290–93.

Haykin, Michael A. G. *Kiffin, Knollys and Keach: Rediscovering Our English Baptist Heritage*. Leeds: Reformation Today Trust, 1996.

Hays, Brooks, and John E. Steely. *The Baptist Way of Life*. Englewood Cliffs, NJ: Prentice-Hall, 1963.

Howson, Barry H. *Erroneous and Schismatical Opinions: The Questions of Orthodoxy Regarding the Theology of Hanserd Knollys (c. 1599–1691)*. Leiden: Brill, 2001.

Ivimey, Joseph. *A History of English Baptists*. 4 vols. London: printed for the author, 1814.

———. "A Wonderful Appearance of Providence at Baptism." *The Baptist Magazine* 10 (1818) 257.

Jewitt, Llewellynn. *A History of Plymouth*. Plymouth: W. H. Luke, 1873.

Lumpkin, William L. *Baptist Confessions of Faith*. Rev. ed. Valley Forge, PA: Judson, 1969.

Martin, Hugh. "The Baptist Contribution to Early English Hymnody." *The Baptist Quarterly* 19/5 (January 1962) 195–208.

Martin, John. *Some Account of the Life and Writings of the Rev. John Martin*. London: n.p., 1797.

Nicholson, Henry M. *Authentic Records Relating to the Christian Church Now Meeting in George Street and Mutley Chapels, Plymouth: 1640 to 1870*. London: Elliot Stock, 1904.

———. *A History of the Baptist Church Now Meeting in George Street Chapel, Plymouth from 1620*. London: Baptist Union, 1904.

Nuttall, Geoffrey F. "Abingdon Revisited, 1656–1675." *The Baptist Quarterly* 36/2 (April 1995) 96–103.

"Original Letters." *The Congregational Magazine* 11 (January 1828) 23.

Pike, G. Holden. "A Western Pastor in the Olden Time." *The Sword and the Trowel* (September 1, 1870) 404–11.

Rippon, John. *The Baptist Annual Register*. Vol. 3. London, 1793–1802.

Smith, George. "Devonshire." *The Evangelical Magazine and Missionary Chronicle* 33 (September 1861) 640.

Spence, H. D. M. *The Church of England*. London: Cassell, 1898.

Venner, Thomas. *The Last Speech and Prayer with other Passages of Thomas Venner*. London: n.p., 1660.

White, B. R. "Cheare, Abraham (1626–1668)." In *Biographical Dictionary of British Radicals in the Seventeenth Century*, edited by Richard L. Greaves and Robert Zaller. Brighton, UK: Harvester, 1983–1984.

———. "Early Baptist Letters (I)." *The Baptist Quarterly* 27/4 (October 1977) 148.

———. *The English Baptists of the Seventeenth Century*. Didcot, UK: Baptist Historical Society, 1996.

———. "John Pendarves, the Calvinistic Baptists, and the Fifth Monarchy." *The Baptist Quarterly* 25/6 (April 1974) 251–72.

———. "The Organisation of the Particular Baptists, 1644–1660." *The Journal of Ecclesiastical History* 17/2 (October 1966) 1–12.

White, W. H. K. *West-Country Poets: Their Lives and Works*. London: Elliot Stock, 1896.

Whitley, W. T. *Congregational Hymn-Singing*. London: J. M. Dent, 1933.

Wilson, Walter. *The History and Antiquities of Dissenting Churches and Meeting Houses*. 4 vols. London: n.p., 1801–1808.

Woolrych, Austin. *Britain in Revolution: 1625-1660*. Oxford: Oxford University Press, 2004.

Worth, R. N. *History of Plymouth From the Earliest Period to the Present Time*. Plymouth: William Brendon, 1890.

www.ingramcontent.com/pod-product-compliance
Lightning Source LLC
Chambersburg PA
CBHW070631220426
R18178600001B/R181786PG43193CBX00011B/11